THE ROOM

by John M. Brewer, Jr.

The Room
John M. Brewer Jr.

One Monkey Books
156 Diamond Street
San Francisco, CA 94114

OneMonkeyBooks.com
Publisher@OneMonkeyBooks.com

Contact the author at gpcramseysoral@aol.com

ISBN: 978-0-9777082-4-6

Contents

'House Don't Move

For as long as I breathe I will remember the late August morning I first walked down that narrow hall and entered that dirty gray door. It was still a few weeks before classes would start for my ninth grade year at Westinghouse High. I'd rushed through breakfast, my mother complaining about how fast I ate.

"Boy, what *are* you doing! You act like some wild animal from Tarzan."

"Naw, Mom." I wiped the maple syrup off my mouth and headed away from the table.

"I don't think all this running around to play football is right, John. Just wait until your father comes home." She fixed a hand on her hip.

"Dad told me I could try out," I said.

She dried her hands on her yellow apron and followed me into the living room. She reached for the big black Bible on the mantle and flipped slowly through some pages.

"What about your heart murmur, son?"

I fidgeted with my belt buckle trying to remember exactly what our family doctor had said. "Dr. Greenlee said I could, right? Right, Mom?"

"Dr. Greenlee played school football with your father," she reminded me. "He would love to see you play. But look at his kids. They're smart. They don't play sports. He is just trying to relive his childhood. Maybe you should take up tennis or golf lessons!"

I was turning the front door knob. "What tennis? That game is for cream puffs! I can just see me dancing down the alley with a tennis racquet under my arms, asking the guys to play tennis. They would laugh me out of town. Besides, Westinghouse ain't got no tennis team," I laughed, aching to leave.

"Don't get smart with me, boy!" she declared, pointing to her yearbook on the shelf. "You don't know how much more we were exposed to in school. We had fencing teams, debate teams and other things all the kids—black or white—did together. But since they pushed the white kids out of Homewood...."

"What ya mean 'pushed out'? Dennis and Mike still go there."

"Oh, ask your father. He'll tell you all about those real estate companies sending white homeowners those thirty-day warnings. Scaring all those white folks out of Homewood." Both hands on her hips, she waited for my smart reply, then added, "Why don't you ask someone at school about a safer activity than football?"

"Oh sure Mom, sword fighting like Zorro is real safe," I responded without thinking.

She threw her hands up in the air, then waved goodbye as I went out. I felt a little bad about how I had talked to her. She was only trying to watch out for me and keep me from getting hurt. Nevertheless, I was free to try out for the team and excited about trying out some of the football moves my mentor, Clyde Hefflin, had taught me earlier that year in the park.

1959. At age 13 I stood about five-foot-six and weighed about 150 pounds (by junior year I would be five-nine and 190), but already my shoulders were broad and my waistline still under 25 inches. My eyes were very dark, my light brown skin tanned browner by the summer sun. My face was round with 69 freckles spread out on both sides of my nose.

Dad saw to it that I kept my hair cut very close. Sometimes he would put a bowl on my head and cut every hair that showed below it. If I was lucky he would let me run down to Hicks barbershop on Frankstown Avenue for a real nice haircut. It was fun to sit in the shop and listen to the tall tales the oldsters would tell. They were the smartest men in the world. Just ask them about anything or anyone and they would talk for a hour. It was like hearing a live sports broadcast from Madison Square Garden way up in New York. I also remembered the fixed look on the faces of the elderly people at the old folks home on Oakwood Street as I dashed by on the way to my first practice. They reminded me of colorful dolls. They hardly ever moved. Only their eyes opened wide as I waved. I think they actually enjoyed watching me run by there every day.

Further down Oakwood was the loud and crazy Circus bar where I always heard men and women swearing and laughing loudly. In front of each one sat a small glass filled with brown liquid. Then someone would heave it into his mouth, jerking his head backwards as he yelled out, "Yeahhhh, that's damn good!"

What I did not understand was why he would also make such a horrible face, like he had been bitten by Godzilla. If it was so *good*, why did they make such horrible faces? I never had time to stop and ask.

I continued past Jackie Miles' house on Kelly Street. Her parents' yard had nicely shaped bramble bushes, just begging me to high-jump over without getting stuck by the thorns. Some days I made it, other days not. Anyhow, it was good practice and I thought would toughen me up to play ball.

The ultimate test was just a few blocks away down Frankstown near the 913 Club. I stopped and took a short break at the corner of Frankstown and Braddock Avenues. Just a few feet in front of me was my special obstacle course. It was four city blocks of streetcar barns on Frankstown. Each barn was open on both ends. Within those four blocks, my only escape from the workers inside was three small side streets that cut across Frankstown. Running through the barns had started as a "dare you" from my friend Skippy Hayes.

"I dare you, man, to run through. Those white guys will beat you up. Ain't no Negroes working inside. You don't have a prayer if they catch you," he'd said.

"Then they got to catch me first, Skip," I said, taking a deep breath and pulling up my jeans.

I ran inside the first car barn. Old-fashioned trolley cars were parked against the far wall. My shoes slipped on some trolley tracks coated with grease. This barn was pretty dark. I only saw one worker, half-asleep on an old milk crate.

That barn was a good warm-up challenge. The second was something different. There were overhead cranes, small pits in the floor, dozens of trolley tracks and a large crew of men throwing tools around. I quickened my pace before they realized I was there.

Suddenly someone yelled, "Hey, you sneak, what you doing in here?"

The other workers stopped and turned.

"Git the hell out of here, punk!" a fat guy hollered, tossing a wrench.

I started to sprint, ducking the flurry of objects aimed to take my head off. I could see daylight coming from the next side street. I was excited and scared at the same time. My T-shirt felt heavy, drenched in sweat. I skipped the side street exit and ran on to the final two barns. A few men were painting trolleys or cleaning their insides. Rusted streetcar rails lay scattered loose across the floor. Before I knew it I was out the last car barn, safe again on the street outside.

"Wow! What a rush!" I shouted, thinking, *Got to do this every day.*

That hot August morning, no longer just one of the junior high kids, ready to accept the challenge of football at Westinghouse High, I felt brave in a new kind of way.

I arrived along the front of the school, near an underpass between the main school building and the more recent addition through which, in junior high, I had been forced to enter. An arched walkway linked the two buildings, and underneath the arch was a dark, tunnel-like passage that led down to our one athletic field behind the school. So far, I had learned three things about that underpass. First, it was seldom lighted and a great spot to maybe kiss a girlfriend. Second, only ball players, coaches, student trainers, and the cleanup men were expected to use it. Third, it was a fine place to go if you wanted to get the mess scared out of you.

"Hey, kid," a red-headed white man with a clipboard yelled from the mouth of the tunnel. "What the hell you going to do? Play ball or count the dandelions?"

"Yes sir," I answered. "I'm going to play ball for The 'House! Where can I sign up?"

Somehow familiar, he smiled and led me into the tunnel. Part way through, he pointed to a door and motioned me to go inside. "You just walk straight, son, you'll see."

It was some kind of back, secret passage to the gym. Spooky. Still. Behind us, outside the underpass, even the late summer locusts were quiet. Ahead, down that dark, gray hall, the air had a funny smell like nothing I had smelled before. A thought of trap doors ran a chill up my back. As I stepped inside, I turned to ask the man with the clipboard what was making the smell, but to my surprise he was gone, vanished.

I was heading slowly alone down the hall when I heard strange voices chanting, "Hey now, hey now," like voodoo or some ritual cult. I froze and sharpened my ears. The chanting grew louder. I rubbed the sweat from my forehead. Maybe I was in the wrong place. Maybe I was also afraid to find out what lay just around the next bend in the hallway. Suddenly someone or something grabbed my shoulder from behind. I flinched, spun, and raised my fist.

"Hey, hold up, man," said a small, skinny kid in shorts. "Be cool, man. What are you doing here?"

"I'm here to play ball for The 'House."

"Oh, yeah!" he shouted. "My name is Pete. They call me Little Pete. I'm one of the trainers. Everyone gets their equipment from me," he added proudly.

I lowered my arm.

"Why all that weird chanting?" I asked. "And what is that weird smell?"

Little Pete bent over to adjust a strap securing a brace on his knee. "That's coming from The Room, my man. Don't you know about The Room, boy?"

I stood there clueless.

"Do you mean to tell me you ain't heard about all them young bloods getting their bones crushed, teeth smashed, and pretty faces pushed in? Well, do you?" He seemed ready to launch into stories.

"Why yeah, Pete," I headed him off. "I heard some tales. But who believes Bubbles and Flip?"

Bubbles and Flip were two guys who spent all their time on the steps beside the playground at Baxter elementary, another nearby school, telling funny stories imitating that fictitious, crazy pair of brothers—Dolomite and Shine—that black kids would rap about at the time.

Pete turned serious. "You best believe them stories about The Room—for your own good. I used to be the fastest kid on the junior squad, man."

"Something happen to your leg? Get hit by a car?" I asked.

"Yeah, it was something, all right. But it wasn't no car. It happened in there."

I stared at an old gray door a little further down the hall. As I did, another door slammed behind along the wall and Little Pete was gone. For a moment I stood there, dazed, then moved on down the corridor to the gym, where the sign-up was going on. Ahead of me, two very short lines of boys stood facing a table.

"Where is everybody else?" I wondered. "Am I early?"

"Next! Next!" The red-headed man motioned to me. "I said *Next*! You still dreamin', kid?"

"No sir, just waiting my turn to sign up. I'm ready to play ball," I said proudly.

He glanced over his black-rimmed glasses. "Full name, son."

"I'm John Brewer, sir."

"Right. Couple years ago, won the forty-yard-dash for Crescent grade school, didn't you?"

"How did you know?" I asked. Somehow I still didn't quite recognize the Westinghouse assistant coach, Wesley Dennis, who had spoken to me way back at that grade school meet.

"It's my business, kid. Sign here." He pointed to the bottom of a form. "Go back to the equipment window and get your mouthpiece and pads."

I walked back along the hall where Little Pete had disappeared on me a few minutes before. It was one of those "Dutch doors" he'd gone behind, and the top half of the door was open. He stood behind the lower panel, football equipment behind him. Now he was business-like, holding out some shoulder pads and white football jersey and pants.

"If the pants don't fit, pull 'em up. This is all we got," he said.

Other tryouts were standing around. My friend Skippy Hayes was there. That was good because he and I had pledged to stick together no matter what happened. Skippy lived on Singer Place, one street up the hill from my house on Oakwood. Instead of a street, a long, steep staircase ran up the hill from my house to his. It was part of what we called the "city steps," a series of block-long staircases—maybe five hundred steps in all—that ran from Oakwood at the base to a high point three or four blocks above. Those stairs had linked our paths together since first grade. Skippy was taller than me, but his medium-brown body was not particularly muscled. At school he wore thick, dark-rimmed glasses and carried a briefcase. In fact, he looked like he could have been the son of a professor.

But Skippy was very strong despite his appearance, and he weighed about 170. I had seen him pick up a boulder that took two other guys to move. He would push his long body back and forth with always a serious look on his face. He also spoke strangely, from the back of his mouth. Usually the first sounds out of his mouth were like the grunts and groans of some old man.

"Huh! Huh! Keep your cool, Brew," he called me by one of my various nicknames as we entered the now open door to The Room, followed by other recruits.

I stepped down into what looked like a dungeon. A strange smell rushed into my nostrils, stronger than the smell in the hall or back in the gym.

"Whew! It stinks in here," someone said behind me.

"Smells like blood and guts," a short kid beside me remarked.

We collected in the empty middle of the room, just looking around. There wasn't much to see but wooden benches, hooks along the walls, and showers down at one end.

"GET THE HELL OUT OF THE CIRCLE, PUNKS!"

The voice exploded in our ears. We moved back, heads down, looking for a line. We backed up all the way to the concrete wall and pinned ourselves against it searching for some sign of a circle. But there wasn't any we could see—no circle, no line, no nothing to move away from. One of the senior players came toward us from the back of the room.

"Scrubs, you get one warning. I'm Timbo, and I'm going to tell you one time."

This Timbo looked scary—a good six-two, eyes deeply sunk in his tan-skinned head. Cheek bones sharply chiseled. He looked like some Cro-Magnon caveman. He certainly got our respect in a hurry.

"NEVER, BUT NEVER, WALK INSIDE THIS CIRCLE OR YOU WILL GET 42 TOWELS FOR SURE."

He pointed to what must have been an imaginary circle in the middle of the floor.

I looked from him to the floor and then to the other "scrubs" Around me, recognizing several others. One was Kenny Lewis, a kid who lived on Maderia Street, close to my house. He was well over six-foot, dark-skinned, with a large, wide-nosed head and thick, black curly hair. Kenny was one of the larger kids in our small band of recruits.

Next to him was Eugene Minard, definitely the smallest tryout for the team. Minard could not have weighed more than

109 and was barely five feet tall. A short while later, as I was slipping into my baggy uniform, I watched him put on four layers of socks to make his thin legs appear larger.

He better be really fast, I thought.

We finished changing for practice, then marched slowly out, avoiding that invisible circle. Moments later we all stood at the top of a flight of concrete steps that led down a steep slope to the field. The upper part of the slope was grass. Lower down, eight or ten rows of bleachers were built into the hillside. Some people were hanging out on them, apparently to watch the practice. We stood there inhaling the soft summer breeze and sweet, distant sweet of Nabisco bread from the factory half a mile away across from Mellon Field on the edge of the neighboring East Liberty district of Pittsburgh.

We began to descend. The "field" was bare of vegetation, just a firmly compacted black-brown dirt slicked over with oil to keep down the dust. You could see and feel the heat waves rising from the oil.

"Looks like 'Death Valley Days,'" Minard whispered.

We snickered. The Bulldogs were already down there doing push-ups in a circle. They stopped to look at us and laugh.

"You in the pot, now, boy!"

"Look at them pretty boys."

They kept up the talk as the circle enlarged to include us. They started jumping-jacks in place. We followed.

They started to chant—"'House don't move, 'House don't move, 'House don't move"—clapping and never missing a beat. Every pair of football spikes hit the field at the same time, hard. Chanting with joy and excitement, we sounded like a well-rehearsed band, no pain, our bodies invaded by the spirits of champions past from the great tradition of *'House-don't-move.*

Two players jogged into the center. The first had number 47 printed on his practice shirt. He was white with blond curly hair. His face was clean-shaven, fully exposing a large dimple on his chin. We soon discovered he was one of the two team captains—the "Blond Bomber," Mike Bisceglia, starting full-back.

The second team captain was left guard Teddy Harris, called "Mr. Clean" because of his brown, round bowling- ball head, bald like the head on a bottle of detergent. Teddy looked very serious. His lips knit tightly together below an exceptionally wide nose. His jersey was 56.

Blond Bomber and Mr. Clean increased the pace and encouraged everyone to shout out louder and clap. We went on playing follow the leader, ignoring the heat. A few of my fellow scrubs slowed down. Skippy motioned for me to look to my right, where a real chubby kid we all knew as "Big George" had twice already almost stopped.

"Pick them feet up, fat boy!" Mr. Clean hollered.

Big George was struggling just to stand up. His arms were barely moving. His feet lifted off the ground only by an inch or so. We all expected him to collapse.

"Come on, fat boy, we seen you jump into the donut shop last week," a player hollered across the circle, while others laughed at poor George.

"All right, team, let's do some push-ups."

Mr. Clean dropped to the tar, stretched out. Instead of placing each hand firmly flat on the dirt, he hoisted his entire body up supported by the fingertips. This new style of push-up was not at all like what Mr. Hartman had taught us back at Crescent. We had to rest every pound on the tips of ten skinny finger? And Teddy wanted each push-up *sloooow*.

"Up!" he demanded and made us hold our weight in the air.

"Down!" He lowered toward the ground, warning us not to rest our bodies there. "Don't get those pretty shirts dirty. Hey, Moose! Check them scrubs' shirts out after we do these finger-tips. If you find even a speck of dirt on them, all the scrubs will have to repeat this drill."

"Sure will, Mr. Clean," replied a guy whose jersey was tattooed *Moose*. "Be glad to see who cheated."

We tried to keep pace with Mr. Clean. One by one we dropped like flies, face first to the oil. Two new guys fainted. One rolled around crying. We all were going to be penalized later. I made it to fifty-two before I hit the hard, hot dirt.

"All right, scrubs, line up for some wind sprints." Teddy pointed toward the end of the field.

"I got a line here," somebody hollered.

Five more lines formed as the chanting continued. "Hey, now! Hey, now!" we shouted and somehow managed to get back in the groove again.

Assistant coach Dennis—I had finally realized who he was—appeared with a whistle fixed in his mouth.

"All right, you know the drill! Line 'em up and move out when you hear the whistle," he ordered.

Timbo pointed at us. "No doggin' it, scrubs."

Before we knew it, the older players in the six lines started to dart back and forth within their line, arranging themselves abreast of certain other guys. The scrubs were pushed from line to line, then shuffled back or forward in line to where the older ones said we should be. It looked like we were arranged in heats to be running against five other guys who might play some position similar to our own. Seconds later the first whistle blew. The six heads of line were all the big linemen. They took off running against each other, heading full-speed downfield. The second whistle blew, and six smaller linemen were off to the races.

By now, I was third in my line. I looked side to side to see who I would be running against. All my opponents were senior players of various sizes and shapes. Mean Moose was standing next to me, about six-foot-two, number 88 on his knee pads. Another player was a guy named Willy Hancock I remembered seeing on the corner of Tioga and Rosedale, standing near an old gas station. His younger sister, Barbara, and I had been in some classes together at Crescent. To my left, none other than Mr. Clean himself had jumped in my heat. That made me nervous.

I took a deep breath. This was my chance to earn some respect. The heat before ours hunched into position. Their whistle blew and they took off. I began to get set, but the whistle blew again before I was ready to run. The other five players took off in a pack. I pushed myself to catch up. Twenty-five yards down the field I caught them, then passed them all, ten yards before we reached the goal line. I wheeled around to greet them with a slight smile face, expecting them to slow down as they barreled toward me.

Arms and elbows raised, they wiped out my grin with a barrage of blows to the head, chest, neck, and shoulders, tossing me backward in the air like an unwanted teddy bear. I tumbled several times head over end before my body came to rest. My eyes were running. A small but steady stream of blood ran from my nose to the ground.

Dazed, I thought, *Maybe I'm dead and just don't know it.*

I was probably not out for long. Pretty soon it seemed like the voices were becoming louder. At least, my sense of hearing was waking again. One voice became very clear.

"You yellow punk! Think you're cute, trying to make us look bad?" Moose shouted as he and the other players looked down at me. "Want some more, punk?"

The other four laughed and adjusted their pads. I felt betrayed, hurt, embarrassed to even look up. Why would they hurt me because I was fast? I was sure Coach Dennis would come to my rescue, but he was nowhere in sight, like he'd disappeared into the wood. Slowly I gained enough energy back to pull myself up off the ground. The other scrubs looked as shocked as I was. The oily scrapes on my bare legs started to burn.

"Get up, scrub!" Moose yelled again. "Get back in line."

I could barely stand, but I managed, ready to quit then and there. *What about your heart murmur, son?* I could hear my mother say. But how could I face Dad if I quit? He would never have quit or let any person beat him down.

Moose shoved his fingers in my face. "You deaf, punk? I said get back in line."

The blood in my mouth somehow revived me. I trotted back down the field to rejoin the line, ignoring the blood and the stinging pain from various parts of my body. Moose's shouts barely reached me.

"Hey, now! Hey, now!" I shouted myself. "Let's do it again!"

A whistle blew. Everyone on the field simply froze in their tracks. The whistle kept on screaming like a train was barreling onto the field. All heads turned to face the top of the rise on our right. Every player's eyes were fixed on a figure standing high above us at the top of the concrete steps.

"Huh! Coach Reno," Skippy muttered my way.

"Who?"

"Head coach! Reno Cesare! He's the man, the legend."

Coach Reno began his descent from the height, planting each leg slowly downward, like the King of England strutting down to command his subjects. He never took his eyes off us. The players began to draw together, as though this giant white magnet were making them move.

He made his way down the last seven steps, then stopped. He looked like a large white bulldog. His thick lips were open, fixed like that, cheeks drooping from his jaw. His eyes were midnight black, small, with bags in his cheeks. His skin looked worn a milky white. For a moment he looked toward some kids in the bleachers.

"Hey, coach, what you got this year?" a big kid yelled.

Coach's words rushed out of that bulldog mouth: "Why are you sitting in the stands? Afraid your pretty face might get bruised?"

The stands went wild with laugher as the big kid dropped his head.

"The boys are lookin' good, coach," hollered another.

"We'll see!" he barked back, stepping onto the field. He was neatly dressed in a blue, short-sleeve jersey with a Bulldog emblem over his heart.

"All right, Wesley, let's see what they got!" He pointed at the grassy slope above the bleachers. "Give 'em the hill."

We were all still exhausted from the exercises and sprints in the 98-degree sun, our uniforms drenched with sweat, as they herded us up to the foot of what looked like a Mount Everest of tall, slippery grass. Standing by a wide concrete drain between the bleachers and the upper slope, we could hardly see the top.

"Keep those helmets on!" Moose shouted from the field.

Skip and I gasped for air.

"Damn, Brew, man," Big George whined. "I can't make it, man, I'm gonna die."

"Just pace yourself, big boy," said Minard.

"Shit," said Big George. "Easy for you to say. You only a hundred pounds. I'm too fat to climb."

"Show 'em how it's done, Spider!" Coach Dennis ordered.

Out of the blue, a short, well-built kid, "Spider" Webb, sped up from the field and dashed up the slope without breaking a sweat, short brown legs never breaking stride. Amazed, we watched this kid run up and down that slippery hillside.

Big Kenny Lewis sort of laughed and said, "Yeah, easy for him. He's a damn spider with twenty legs."

We all tried to laugh it off as Spider made back-to-back demonstration runs up to the top. At the top of his second run, he stopped, held up a white rag and motioned for us to go when he dropped it. It fell and we started to run up the hill. The grass was wet but we dug in our spikes. The slope was severe. I could feel myself slowing down. At least two other scrubs had reached the same height as I had, but the rest were halfway down behind us. Big George was at the rear of the pack.

Finally we all reached the top. Spider told us to head back down. We went down wordless, slipping and falling.

"Okay, let's do it again," he said.

We all bent over to catch a breather. Big George and his buddy, Ron Bush, both heaved on the bleachers. Skippy's eyes were almost out of his bald head. My stomach went into cramps.

"They tryin' to kill us," said Kenny.

"Come on, big guy, Kendow, pump them long legs." It was one of us, little Minard, challenging Kenny.

Chester Slaughter, my closest friend among the tryouts, had given Kenny that nickname "Kendow" for some odd reason some time ago. And from that first day Chester was always renaming other fellow scrubs. He called Larry Berry "Block" because of Larry's square-shaped muscles. Jon Henderson, our scrub quarterback, was nicknamed "Hindu," which sounded cooler than Henderson. One of the white scrubs, Sonny, we called "Rabbit" because of the shy way he walked. Elmer Goodson had the nickname "Bootsey," which I think he'd got from one of the many girls that liked him. George Harris was "Big George" because of his girth. Me, on the team I became known known as "Bronco" for my style when I ran the ball.

The regular players, we were learning, all had nicknames as well. There was "Eddie Fye-eddie," "Moose," "Johnny Hop," "Train," "Sticky," "Thunder," and other wild-sounding monikers, handed out long before Chester arrived. Now we were looking up the hillside at "Spider" who was about to make our lives even more unbearable by dropping that damn white rag again.

We started up again, groaning and grunting. Two simply passed out and rolled back down the hill into the concrete drain. One kid tossed his helmet off, ran off the hill, and never showed up at another practice. The heat, the pain were unbearable. My throat was too dry to spit. I just kept climbing until I got there.

Very few of us made it to the top that second time. Hardly anyone made it the third and fourth. Bodies were spread all over the hill, pushed beyond limits, embarrassment, shame, or concern over who witnessed our failure. We lay in piles, aching, limp, lifeless, mangled, and twisted around each other, panting a unison animal sound. Some guys were crying. Others were dazed. No one could talk. We were in a state one level higher than pain. It was like watching yourself fall from the Larimer Avenue Bridge, which crossed the ravine between Pittsburgh's Homewood and its East Liberty district, knowing you die when you hit the potholed boulevard below—unless a plea to God could save you.

That first day of practice ended with at least half of us praying to Jesus. The other half quit and went about their business, never to return. Those of us who decided to return the next day knew there was a lot more to come.

We had no idea.

Steel City Justice

If this story is all about justice, it comes from my dad. Especially where his family was concerned, when things got out of line, John M. Brewer, Sr., showed no fear about putting them right.

As a younger kid in the early fifties I had loved to play soccer and dodgeball on the "red dog"—red clay and cinder—field at Crescent School every afternoon. I could kick the ball halfway down the field, was pretty fast, and would run until I was ready to drop. All my friends played—Little Bill Evans, Mark Prunty, Bobby Beverly —plus the two local bullies, Pete and Billy Scott. Whenever Pete was losing, he'd start to punch us around. He was almost fifteen and larger than any other kid in our games. I tried many times to stand up to him—and took my lumps. I don't think I ever complained about the Scott brothers at home, but it never surprised me that Dad knew about the many times they whipped our butts. He always seemed to know what was going on in my life.

One day after school, he came home in his black Ford from his work in Pittsburgh's Lower Hill, with two of the toughest kids I had ever laid eyes on. Not big but very tense and mean. He called one Jimbo, the other Bill.

The Scott brothers were sitting down the alley. Dad pointed them out. Like a pair of panthers, these young Hill cats exploded past our softball game. The brothers must have seen them coming. They ran into their backyard and into their house. But that didn't stop Dad's terrible twosome. They plunged right through the Scotts' back door. We stood with our mouths wide open, hearing the Scott brothers' screams and pleas.

Moments later, Jimbo and Bill calmly walked out of the house and jumped back in Dad's car. They never said a word, and the Scott brothers never touched us again.

From that day on, I knew Dad would always protect the underdog regardless of the odds, and he became my real-life hero. I always suspected that TV heroes like Hop-a-Long Cassidy, Superman, and even Zorro, my first black hero, were not real. But Dad was real.

He was a big, muscular, evenly brown man, though not what most considered tall, which may be why I was never tall either. I would often see him in a sleeveless undershirt and would check out the large muscles of his arms with huge veins popping out. He had a horseshoe engraved on the left arm that he proudly flexed around his twin brother, James, when family came to see us. I could never figure Dad for a tattoo, but that horseshoe sure looked like one. I knew from other older people that Dad had once been a football player, maybe a boxing champ as well. Every time some older person asked my name, next question would be, "Do you play ball like your daddy and Uncle James?" It sounded like the Brewer twins had been great athletes back in the old days.

Dad seemed to have his place in the world. By the time I was nine or ten, I was pretty much aware he was a gym teacher in the Lower Hill, a hard-scrabble part of Pittsburgh, close to downtown. That's where he'd recruited Jimbo and Bill to set things right with the Scotts. I often wondered why he wasn't teaching closer to home, but he really loved teaching what he called the "knuckle heads" down at Vann School. In a few more years, he would step up from teaching, into a principal's shoes.

Dad handled some of the meanest black kids in the Hill. He taught them back flips, wrestling, and even some gymnastics. What he did not have to teach them was how to fight. From conversations between my parents, I surmised that kids there led some pretty hard lives. They fought all the time and could handle themselves, even on those wild streets.

We lived five or six miles out, on the eastern end of Pittsburgh, in an area called Homewood-Brushton, but sometimes Dad took me down to The Hill to look at the smoking mills that lined the brown Monongahela River.

In the mid-1940s when I came on the scene, those mills were America's war-making machine. People a little older than I am remember the wartime days around my birth when the sunlight never broke through. They carried umbrellas as shields from the soot. In those days, only the milkman wore white. Everyone else wore sad, dull shades that wouldn't show the grit.

In the later forties and early fifties, steelmaking still meant everything to the families of Pittsburgh. From along its rivers, smokestacks like giant cigars still puffed out tons of grit that settled everywhere across the city's hills, ravines, and byways.

Back in those days, to my young eyes, big things seemed to be happening, and everyone seemed so involved in whatever they were pursuing. Near where we lived, I remember the mill workers climbing aboard the old streetcars in their matching brown or gray pants and shirts, shiny aluminum lunch boxes wedged proudly under their arms. Here and there you might see a gold chain displayed from a belt loop, neatly disappearing into a front pocket where a wind-up pocket watch hid. They just could not wait for you to ask the time of day.

"Half past seven," they would say after pulling it out and flipping it open, a look of delight on their worn faces. It was as if they lived for that moment of recognition.

Day after day they rode that pale, red-and-white trolley down Fifth Avenue the five or six miles to what everyone knew as "the steel mill guys' stop." At that other end we sometimes watched them, one by one, stepping down on the pavement at Fifth and Kirkpatrick. Like football players on the lip of a stadium, they'd stand there, motionless, staring at the stacks of J&L Steel across the Brady Street Bridge on the south side of the Monongahela. A few minutes later they'd be across and entering the gates of enormous black sheds. What challenges would they face that day? Men got killed in the mills. We had heard the horrible stories, the accidents in that J&L "hell hole" of searing ovens, open flames, lumbering overhead cranes, and acres of metal scattered across the mill's dirt floors.

You could hear the morning shift horn for miles. The shift gates opened wide and men marched in to the same ugly tasks as the day before. No beginning or end to the work. No escape from the foul, polluted atmosphere or scorching furnace heat.

Eight hours later, another blast of the shift horn meant return to the streets of the South Side, to the thousand "beer-and-shot" joints conveniently located steps from the mill. Several rounds might wash the nauseating taste of sulfur from their mouths. A short while later we would see them back at Fifth and Kirkpatrick, boarding the outbound trolley: white or brown faces grit-darkened to black; only their eyes looked clean. They looked like two-legged raccoons. If I and my friends were hanging around there, we'd snicker as they climbed aboard.

But whatever they looked like, same as Dad they had their place—their role to play in this city. Every day he, too, would climb out of bed, kiss me on the forehead as I pretended to remain asleep, and go, returning home by supper time, exhausted, to our house on Oakwood Street.

How fortunate I was to even have a Dad at home, a luxury most of my friends went without. They all seemed to have a mom or grandmother living with them instead. "Little John" Wilson did have a dad we would often see standing in front of the carwash on Bennett Street near Crescent School. He was a short, dark man whose belly hung over his pin-striped trousers. Little John called him "Dee-De."

Dee-De used to pull the elastic on his red suspenders as he bit down on an unlit cigar. His hair was intensely conked with grease. John always hit him up for pennies for us to invest in jelly donuts from the nearby donut shop. Dee-de was happy to give us the pennies to get rid of our small crew of boys, but I never saw him at John's house; he must have lived elsewhere.

John's mother was always on the run. She dressed really flashy with a tight skirt and pink blouse that pushed everything to the top of her brown, shapely frame. Her hair was neatly pressed and waved in the back. Mrs. Wilson never had to walk or take a trolley car. Every evening, some real cool guy would pick her up in a red Cadillac convertible. She must have made good money at her job because Little John was always dressed in the latest style. I used to see her coming home at 6:00 a.m. as I made my paper route rounds.

"Morning, Mrs. Wilson," I would holler—sometimes twice to catch her attention.

She would slowly stop and turn her head as she climbed the steep steps to her house. Slowly she would tip her dark glasses down from her eyes and say, "Oh, hi, Butch." She always sounded a little fatigued. "How's yo mom?"

"Fine, she fixing breakfast for my brother Norman."

"Yo dad still teachin' school?" she'd say, two or three steps from her porch.

"Dad's gone to work already," I'd answer politely and continue down Oakwood toward the first place on my route.

I was lucky to have a mother at home, too. Unlike Little John's, mine never had to work outside the house. Mom never wore flashy clothes or sunglasses in the middle of the night to hide her eyes. She was a light-skinned, small, but shapely woman who had control over the house—that is, until Dad came home. Her close friends, like Aunt Eunice, called her "Pippy."

I always chuckled when I heard that nickname. And I was puzzled why Dad's mother always called him Bill, when his real first name was John, like mine. At some point my grandmother Brewer explained to me that the "Bill" was short for "Bouncing Bill." Back when the twins had been born, babies were born at home in the bedroom. As the story goes, Dad was the first twin to come out, but the doctor felt no signs of life, so he simply tossed Dad toward the edge of the bed as he prepared to deliver the second twin, James. Moments later Dad bounced off the bed and started to cry. So that's how he became "Bouncing Bill." But I never did figure out why they called Mom Pippy.

Our home was part of a red brick duplex, connected to Mr. and Mrs. King's half which was up on a terrace. My white friends lived in brick homes like mine, but many of my black friends lived in wood-framed houses. I always knew there was a difference. Granny pointed it out by repeating the story about the three pigs and what each pig had used to build his house. I sometimes felt a little guilt that I lived in a brick home when some of my friends endured the cold of winter or heat of summer in less well constructed homes. I often wondered if we were rich.

Eight feet over from us was another duplex, one unit of which was occupied by the Ratcliffs. Mr. Ratcliff worked at the Negro newspaper, the *Pittsburgh Courier*. Mrs. Ratcliff was a teacher. They had two kids, Roberta and Mike, but neither wanted to play with me and my small band of friends. Mike was very small and almost pretty for a boy. He had long, black, curly hair, parted on the side of his egg-shaped head. His skin was lighter than the skin of my Italian friend, Archie. Roberta looked even whiter than her brother; she had almost no color at all. She never came outside. She spent her spare time after school trying to learn the violin.

Night after night I could hear her mother saying, "No, no, no, let's try it again."

Mrs. Ratcliff was relentless: determined her daughter would learn to play that horrible instrument. Roberta's bedroom window was directly across from mine, and night after night, the horrible squeaking echoed in the narrow space between our houses. Even on weekends, the useless lessons continued.

Finally I decided to act. First, I rolled paper into spitballs and plastered her windows. Then I raided the milk box on their front porch, drank half the glass quart bottle of milk and topped it off again with water. It took them weeks to find out I was doing that. Somehow I thought those crazy acts would make the music lessons stop. I was wrong. But they cancelled milk deliveries and, before I knew it, moved away.

In the early fifties, Crescent was considered a new elementary school. It went on up through sixth grade, and most every kid I knew went there. The exterior bricks were white. The grass around the school was neatly, pleasingly cut. There were ornaments over the entrances. Inside, the hallways were clean and well lit. The gym where we played dodge ball on Wednesday nights had bright, shiny, wooden floors. The staircase to the third floor was wide with a smooth, strong rail we always rode down.

In fifth grade, I had an experimental class called Negro History taught by a sexy white lady named Mrs. Shuttleworth. Gym class was conducted by a red-faced man named Mr. Hartman. The math teacher was Mrs. Harvey, a very tall, striking, black-skinned woman with a big smile. She made math seem easy. I made sure that I was on my best behavior since she knew my father personally. Failure was not an option for me. She would snap if I got "smart." I got my first A+ in math from her.

"John," she would warn me, "you know I know your Dad, and I will call him if you don't straighten up."

That was the ultimate threat. I could just imagine the veins popping out of Dad's head. I toed the line.

Negro History classes were interesting. Compared with the clownish pictures we would see of Negroes in the newspaper or other books, it was strange and odd to see books in this class filled with Negro inventors, educators and even ambassadors. I was fascinated. Just the thought of people who looked like me inside those books made me proud and warm all over. I stuck my chest out as I walked to class with my white buddy, Archie. Archie was my main buddy. He looked Italian in every respect, with super-black, thick hair, pumped to the limit. His skin was as dark as mine year-round. He always wore his shirts rolled up to the top of his hairy arms and kind of sang when he talked. He was a cool guy.

"Hey, Archie," I said once, pulling his shirt, "did you know that peanut butter you been eating since first grade was made by a Negro just like me?"

He stopped, thought for a minute and replied, "That's good, but my people made the first pizza. You like pizza, don't you, man?"

"Why, yeah, man, but only time we get it is at the school picnic at West View Park. We get peanut butter every day."

We laughed and dashed down the hall for gym. Ten minutes later we were shooting baskets with the other kids. Old crewcut Mr. Hartman blew the black plastic whistle he wore around his red neck. He always slobbered as he barked instructions, one word at a time. His face was animated, eyes pitch-black and deep-set in his large head. He was spooky and funny at the same time. He looked right through you before shouting each word from the back of his throat as though trying to purge them from his mind. We thought he must be seeing ghosts. "All right,...boys,...give me...four...lines...right... here." He'd point to the red line on the floor at the end of the gym. "Wind sprints...when...you...hear...the whistle. Down... and back,...boys. Quickly!"

Some of the guys would moan, but I really didn't mind. As I've said, I loved to run. Later that spring Mr. Hartman picked me out to run track for Crescent at the inter-grade-school meets. I won the 40-yard dash at the end of my fifth- or sixth-grade year. It was at the finals that I had met Wesley Dennis, assistant coach of the formidable Westinghouse Bulldogs, who ruled the city football league. In seventh grade, I'd move over to Westinghouse Junior High, and another two years after that I'd be able to go out for serious sports. In the meantime, I still had some painful growing to do and a great first football mentor to meet.

First Training Ground

My final, sixth-grade year at Crescent was full of weird surprises. First, I began having flashes and funny sensations around certain girls. During our music class I sat directly behind a pretty girl named Eleanor whose hair extended down her backside. She smiled all the time and seemed to tolerate me. I made sketches of her—not exactly how she was but how I wanted her to be. The long wavy hair and pretty face were hers for real. I even colored her face with a light brown crayon and sprinkled a few freckles near her nose. More imaginatively, I also added largish lumps on each side of her chest. When it was done, I slipped the drawing to her, hoping for approval.

She turned completely around and said loudly, "I'm not built like this!"

The music teacher stopped mid-speech and looked to see where the commotion was coming from. Eleanor dropped the paper on the floor. How stupid I felt. Here I was completely exposed to everyone. Why had I added those big, pointed breasts? *How stupid!* Maybe the nasty magazines I'd lifted from the variety book and comic shop on Brushton had made me do it.

A stern look crossed the teacher's face.

"John, why don't you come up to the front of the class and give us your music report?" she ordered.

Suddenly, I felt a flash inside my pants. My private part went wild, out of control. The entire class turned to watch me walk to the front. I could not move. I dared not move and expose myself.

Oh Lord, please help me, I thought to myself. *I'm not trying to think bad.* I continued to try and get hold of myself, but the urge continued to rule me.

I'm dead, I can't move, I kept telling myself.

"John, if you're not ready I'll have to give you a failing grade," she concluded. The class began to snicker.

"Sorry," I said.

"Very well, John, report to the vice principal's office right now."

My body remained glued to the chair. I had to think of something to get me off the hook. Suddenly I got the bright idea to faint. *Just fall out on the floor and roll over a couple times. Yeah, that would do it,* I thought.

Slowly I began to rise from the chair, but before I could pull my stunt my body snapped back in control. No more flashes and wild surges.

Thank you, Lord. I felt like I had just been cured of polio.

"Are you okay, John?" the teacher interrupted my brief, inner celebration.

"Why, ah, no, I'm a little sick." I lied.

"Go to the nurse's office, John, and see me when you are feeling better."

She escorted me out the door.

Man, was that a close one, I thought as I walked down the hallway to the nurse. *What is wrong with me?*

This was not the first time, either. It had happened at church last Sunday during the Lord's Prayer. Also when I was standing in line at Islay's ice cream counter two weeks before. I hadn't even been thinking of girls or of the dirty paperbacks Little John had traded me last summer for my Batman and Superman comics.

Who could I talk to? I was too embarrassed to ask my dad or mother. It had been embarrassing enough last year when I'd caught my penis in my zipper and only Mom was home. The pain was so unbearable that I finally broke down and cried "Mom!" She'd rescued me from the pain. But this was different.

I decided to walk down Homewood Avenue to the park near the railroad tracks and try to figure out my problem. Time spent in Homewood Park was always good. Since I'd been little, my parents had taken me there and let me run free. Small buckeye trees surrounded the park. The grounds were covered with green, soft grass. Small hillsides dipped to open fields of four-leaf clover. Yellow dandelions brightened the grounds. Large oak trees spread their umbrellas of shade.

What I've just described was the upper park. Across the tracks from there was Homewood Park field. The short connecting footbridge gave a close-up, bird's-eye view of big east- and west-bound trains.

Life at the field seemed so simple and complete, where everything was free. This had to be where I could solve my personal problems. I sat on the wooden bleachers and gazed out at some older kids playing a serious game of tackle football. No helmets, no real shoulder pads. One kid had football spikes. The rest just wore heavy sweaters, blue jeans and skull caps.

"Hey! Little man, you want to play?" A tall kid motioned to me to join them.

His football shirt had the number 45 stenciled on the back. He looked at least eighteen years old. He had a small cut on his face that blended into his brown skin.

"Yeah, I'll give it a try," I answered softly.

We played for nearly an hour. The big guys kept tossing me the ball and blocking for me, all the way into the end zone.

As we walked to the water fountain, a pudgy kid called Blue said, "Little boy can hump, can't he, man."

"Hey boy, come here," someone shouted out from sidelines. "I'm Clyde Hefflin, my man, I been watching you."

He was a medium-brown-skinned guy with full lips and a short haircut—compactly built with strong hands, and one big, wide nose. He might have been five years older than me. Not a big guy, but his eyes were intense, and he spoke with authority.

"If you want to learn something about this game, boy, come down to this field every day and I'll teach you. There are some things you got to work on. You got to get your head together, young buck, if you want to do well."

I was totally impressed with him as he continued to tell me his observations. Clyde Hefflin seemed to understand what problems I had to confront. I think he even knew about my special problem of control. Then, as later on, he told me, "Boy, you becoming a man and you got to control that wild animal in your body. Just keep running until that animal lays down."

Before I knew it, I was running home, determined to take his advice. It made sense. *Just run everywhere you go*. So I did. The next morning when I delivered papers, instead of walking my route down Oakwood and up the hill near the old Singer mansion, I dashed, throwing them onto the porches as I ran by. My mind seemed clear. I just knew those wild flashes like the one I'd had in music class would never happen again.

After returning home one morning and inhaling six pancakes, milk and two oranges, I left for school. Quickly I jumped down the concrete steps from porch to sidewalk. I ran down Oakwood past the old folks' home and Circus bar so fast I barely made the turn up a side street near the donut shop. I could smell fresh jelly donuts in the air. Despite this invitation to stop I continued on up Bennett Street, headed toward the car wash. Little John's father was adjusting his suspenders in front of the entrance. He nodded as I ran by.

I was going to be early to school. I had time to visit the large fruit market across the street from Crescent. I thought maybe I could stick an orange in my back pocket.

"Can I help you, boy?" A small white woman appeared out of thin air.

I reached in my pocket and pulled out a dime and a Mary Jane candy wrapper.

"Not enough," I said under my breath.

My grandmother had told me this store's fruit was too high. Seconds later two white men appeared directly behind me.

"You gonna buy something or what, boy?" The taller, bald one asked with a mean look on his red face. The second man just crossed his arms and stared at me.

"No, I mean, no thanks, sir, just lookin'," I replied as I back-pedaled out the open door. This store was like all the stores in Homewood. They really did not like Negro kids, no matter if you had money or not.

It was nearly time for the first bell to ring for school. Soon, I'd end my time at Crescent. Homewood field had become my official training ground and Clyde Hefflin my first real teacher outside school. I felt prepared for what I understood to be the greatest challenge in the City of Pittsburgh: junior high school at Westinghouse High.

Ultimately, my greatest personal challenges at Westinghouse would have to do with football, but there were other challenges as well for me and my friends—black and white—who entered the junior high at that time. The main entrance to the enormous, four-story, gray-black building lay past a black wrought-iron fence and up several concrete banks of steps. Inside the fence on either side of the entrance, the grass was rich, green and cropped like a Sunday picnic lawn. But no junior high student dared go in that way. Like cattle we were made to enter only at the school's north entrance. Once inside, the upperclassmen would often try to beat us down with comments about our age. But these things weighed less heavily on me than on some.

Years before, Westinghouse had had large numbers of both black and white students, but that had begun to shift in the late 1950s as more black families moved into Homewood from parts of The Hill that had been flattened by what the city called "urban development." As I myself entered Westinghouse, a few of my white Catholic friends moved over to parochial school, but my friend Dennis Counahan went to The 'House and we played football there together. Another guy was Danny Iacurci. He also came to Westinghouse and played football there until certain events made him choose to transfer. Even after he left The 'House, he would still come out and hang with us from time to time. In the future Danny and I would be teammates again, under circumstances I could not have imagined.

Cruising Pittsburgh

Around ninth grade, Saturdays were my day to roam free—once my father made sure I had completed the long list of chores my mother had compiled: "Cut the grass... trim the bushes... take the trash out... sweep the steps...." She hardly needed to say it because I just did most all of it before she could open her mouth. I could knock off the bigger chores here and there during the weekdays, so once my morning paper deliveries were done (6:30), I didn't have much more to do, and the day was all mine—at least if my father did not have a repair project lined up for me in the house. In other words, I left pretty early on Saturday mornings and stayed away from home all day until just before the street lights came on.

Some Saturdays I spent hanging out on the block. I gave the guys in the car barn a break from my daily dash through their operations. Usually, I would buy ice cream from Islay's on Homewood Avenue or walk around in the five- and-ten-cent store. By noon my favorite theater, the Belmar, was open and ready to reel through seventeen cartoons before the Saturday double-feature.

Since my weekly allowance from Dad was only fifteen cents and the paper route paid only a few dollars each week, I improvised. Usually my boys and I found a way not to pay for anything at all. We might start at one of the small stores filled with nasty comic books to stare at while we stood there. The old man behind the counter always pointed to a large, black-and-white sign that said *Do Not Touch Unless You Buy.*

We always ignored him and the sign until one day he threatened us with, "Mason the cop is coming to shoot you."

We all had heard stories about Mason, the Negro cop who carried two big six-shooters on his hips. Down at Hicks barbershop they said he would shoot you if you blinked the wrong way. Everybody we knew was afraid of him. But Little John always knew where he was located.

He said, "Mason's in the Hill District. You's lying to us."

Probably his mama had told him that, since she worked somewhere in The Hill with that man in the fancy red car. But we had no fear.

"Let's roll," said Little John one August Saturday morning, around when football practice resumed.

"Let's go up to Baxter school," I suggested. "Play some hoops and take us a dip in the Baxter pool."

"Naw, man," he chuckled, "let's go to East Liberty and see if we can sneak in the movies."

"No, no, no." Bobby Beverly pushed his small arms in the air. "Let's go to The Hill and hang out near one of them night clubs and check them hot chicks out."

Bobby usually attached himself to our small crew, and today it was just him and me and Little John. Bobby's heritage was mixed and his skin so light that some friends of his called him "white Jesus." Despite his small, skinny frame, he was always talking about "getting some." He also had a child-like habit of sticking two fingers of his left hand in his nostrils while sticking the other two in his mouth and resting his long left thumb on his cheek.

"Do you got money to pay for the streetcar?" I asked them both.

"Yeah," John boasted. "Even better, I got some tokens I took from my grandmother's purse."

We used John's tokens to jump on the 88 streetcar from Homewood, on the eastern edge of Pittsburgh, west toward the upper Hill, another largely black community between Homewood and Pittsburgh's downtown. The tokens also got us transfers from the 88 to the 82 car at Frankstown and Lincoln, which would take us the rest of the way. The whole trip down would cost us nothing.

I said upper Hill just now because there were really two parts of the Hill District—lower and upper. The lower one, running down to the river was where I'd watched the steelworkers going to work when I was younger. The upper Hill was above that, naturally. It was really the heart of The Hill.

Between Homewood and there lay East Liberty, a business district where few Negroes worked inside the banks, theatres, jewelry stores, groceries, five-and-tens, or clothing shops, except to cart out boxes at night. East Liberty, like Homewood, had plenty of Negroes shopping in its stores in the daytime, spending money where the "white guys" got all the cash. Neither our own community nor East Liberty seemed to offer us much in the way of real jobs. That seemed to be the general way of Pittsburgh.

But The Hill was different, especially the part that climbed from Schenley High School, westward out Centre Avenue. By the late 1950s, all its stores and joints were run by Negroes and they got all the cash, selling to whites and Negroes. Our tour that day started at the corner of Centre and Kirkpatrick.

Whenever we went, the second we jumped off the 82 Lincoln, loud live music would hit our faces. A drummer's beat joined with a sweet-sounding horn. In summer the air was thick with a harmony of saxophone and wonderful smells like ribs and barbeque chicken. We could taste it all in the air.

Everything moved with the beat. Young children snapped their fingers and switched their heads back and forth. People walked fully upright with a strut never seen in other parts of the city. The men dressed neatly in pleated trousers, colorful shirts and ties. They wore blocked felt hats and fresh hair styles. The ladies wore brightly flowered blouses, slightly open near the top, their womanly shapes poured into tight-fitting skirts inside which their backsides seemed to roam free. Their passing smiles drove us crazy.

This other city, The Hill, was different from Homewood. Here, people did not seem to mind living on top of one another. Apartments were worn down. Living conditions ranged from good to bad. I remembered my Dad once taking me to an old building off Centre. We went in and were led through a tunnel to a large red door. Through that door, I was amazed to see a white carpet, a luxury living room, two pool tables, a bar, and a collection of art like I had never seen before. This place was fresh out of a dream. From there Dad had continued the tour through a maze of connecting joints, luxury pads, and even a small place to eat.

A half-hour later, standing on Wylie Avenue one street up from Centre, he shook hands with and introduced me to a real slick cat named Woogie Harris, standing by a Duesenberg.

Riding home in our own, more ordinary, car, I asked what Mr. Woogie did for a living. By that time Dad had become the city's first Negro principal, at Miller Street School. He smiled and said Woogie and his buddy Gus had made a donation to the school to help buy books and lunches for the kids. He said Woogie saved the lives of hundreds of kids all over the city.

"It's not what you do *for* a living that matters, Butch. It's what you do *with* it," he replied in his normal, indirect way.

I found out later, from Little John, that Woogie was king of the numbers, the illegal betting operation that went on all over the city. People would bet on a number each day, and if that number "hit," they would make back quite a few dollars on the quarter or so they had bet. The Hill was Woogie's headquarters.

Most all of black Pittsburgh depended on these two rich business barons, Woogie Harris and Gus Greenlee. But theirs was a lifestyle very different from my own, the one in which Dad had been raising us up. I became a little concerned that Dad had broken the law by accepting money from "numbers people." Later, he explained how, when he was first appointed principal at Miller, nobody at the school board level expected the school to progress. The staff morale was poor. Some of the books that it had been issued were basically anti-Negro, so what children saw in them were negative images of themselves. Kids at the school were also hungry, near starvation, and couldn't achieve because of that.

Dad told me proudly, "One day I gathered all the negative books and burned them in the outside courtyard. I went to Woogie and Gus Greenlee, as well as others who street-hustled and took up a collection. They recognized these children as their own. Within a year, our achievement levels almost doubled. I reorganized my staff, and now we compete with anyone."

The Hill was indeed a special place, providing me and "my boys" protection. The Hill was a home away from home, where we hung out in packs of three because four or more of us together would make us look like a gang, which was asking for trouble. The usual threesome was me, Kenny ("Kendow") Lewis and his next-door neighbor, Ronnie Roberson. Ronnie always had the money. Kenny had the big, mean look. I was cast in the role of taking the risks.

On the day I've been describing, however, I was down on The Hill with Little John Wilson and Bobby Beverly, two of my friends from the alley. Both were kind of small, so I took on the role of the enforcer. Little John had the money, and Bobby was just there, going along for the ride. As I said before, even at age thirteen, Bobby was still sucking his fingers.

Halfway across Kirkpatrick, Little John turned to Bobby, shouted, "Stop that crap!" and smacked his fingers out of his face.

"Ain't no big thing, John," Bobby protested.

"Yes it is. We in The Hill, boy. We look like some babies walking around!"

I backed up John. With a pissed look, Bobby slid his fingers down in his corduroy pockets.

"We have to blend into what's happening," I told him. "You know, look cool and down, like the rest of these dudes."

"Let's go up Wylie Avenue, man, they may be having a parade or something," Bobby suggested.

"That's the North Side Elks parade, man," I told him. "My old man took me once. They had soldiers from World War II, lady soldiers, marines, navy, army. They had hundreds of drill teams. The girls were super fine, man. But that ain't until later this year."

"Yeah," Bobby agreed. "I heard it is something else. They said the parade was as far as the eye could see."

We looked up Wylie Avenue.

"Told you no parade yet, Bobby," John said.

Bobby smiled and stroked his chin and said, "Let's go down to the Hurricane and see the babes come out."

Little John pointed a finger at Bobby and said, "Is that all you think about, Bob?"

"Hmm, man, let's get a bone!" I said, stopping to face a small rib stand near the curb. I pulled out three quarters and a dollar bill. "How much you got, Little John?"

"I got five, man!" John said. "What 'bout you, lover boy?" he added, pointing at Bobby again.

Bobby kept walking, ignoring our questions, then stopped at the curb by a small grill made from a metal trash can. No one seemed to be watching the grill.

"Hey guys," he said, "ain't nobody here. They got hamburgers, hot dogs, wings. Let's eat for free."

We surrounded the grill and plucked several dogs.

"Where's the buns?" complained John, as Bobby and I started to gorge ourselves. "Damn buns, don't taste right without some mustard and buns."

"That will be two dollars each, boys!" said a voice. "I said, that will be two dollars, boys!"

We looked up and saw a dark blue uniform come out from behind a telephone pole.

"Ahhh, shheet!" hollered John.

It was none other than Mr. Six-Shooter himself, Mason the cop, each long brown hand planted on the butt of a holstered revolver. He just stood there, staring us down with his unblinking, shark-like, lifeless eyes. His chin stuck out like the chin on Dick Tracey, the comic-strip cop.

The tour had just ended. We gave him every penny we had and walked four miles home from The Hill. I was happy to arrive in one piece just seconds before the street lights came on. Another Saturday gone. Sunday would slide quickly by.

By then I was playing Bulldog football, junior varsity squad. Another Monday practice ahead when I'd once again face my real ordeals.

Rabbit and The Knob

Back as far as I knew, Westinghouse had won the city league football championship almost every year, and the fall 1959 football season ended with us on top once again. Our J.V. team matched the success of the big team by winning all its own six city games. Soon, we would be expected to play on the big squad and assume the roles of champions. The older guys began to look at us a lot closer. The real pressure was about to start.

For our part, we looked up to most of those first-team players. And between us scrubs as a whole and the older players as a whole, we seemed to match up nearly the same in terms of potential talent, size and even race. Several Italian kids were now playing first or second string. We scrubs had Sonny, Dennis and Frankie. Dennis played defensive back. He was small, quick, and agile as a panther. Frankie Bisceglia—the scrub younger brother of Blond Bomber Mike who would graduate that June—played offensive guard. He also was not very big but, like Dennis, he was quick and was very determined to get a spot on the roster.

Then there was Sonny, the kid we called "Rabbit." Also a guard, he wasn't big, either, but he had a talent for quietly enduring pain. Rabbit struggled past the drills like everyone else, but never complained. I admired his strength and determination.

All that stood in our way now were a few more months of hazing, we thought. Come August, we would move on up to the varsity team.

"Just stay out of the old guys' way, huh, Brew," Skippy reminded me as we walked past Chick Hales' little soul food joint on Frankstown. "No wearing any good clothes to school. They said wear khaki pants and a light blue shirt with a cheap belt."

"I know, man," I replied. "Kendow told me last week."

"Just think," he went on, eyes growing brighter, "We'll be old guys at the end of next summer. Then you can wear what you want and party anywhere you want."

So most of the winter months of 1960 were spent ducking and dodging the "old guys" in the hallways, lunch room, at the weekly dances at the local YMCA, and even at East Liberty's famous Penn Shady Ballroom. An older street buddy, Delrico Reed, became our official spy, scouting out parties before we made the scene. He also would pitch in with us scrubs on a bottle of "Dirty Bird" wine or Colt 45 beer. Drinking gave us a sense of courage before we hit the streets of Pittsburgh.

A few other friends of mine, like Ronnie Roberson and Kippy French, would hang out with Kendow, Chester and me. Ronnie and Kippy had quit trying to be Bulldogs months before. I think Ronnie quit because of his love of fine clothes. The thought of someone making him wear khakis every day made him sick. As for Kippy, his folks were not too happy about his playing ball for The 'House, and they were transferring him out of the city somehow to play football at Penn Hills High. What had sealed his fate was gettting caught, along with some others of us, in a stolen car. Lucky for us, the thief admitted to the police he had only picked us up as "hitch-hikers."

Winter vanished as the smell of spring flowers began to fill the air. We still attended occasional meetings in The Room conducted by the team captains. We even met at the YMCA and ran plays.

High school football coaches were not permitted to start practice sessions until late August, but Coach Reno Cesare set the tone for these "unofficial" but mandatory spring practices, by saying smugly, "Boys, football season is never over. You gotta think, eat, sleep, drink, and talk football regardless if it's January or July."

"We are the Westinghouse Bulldogs. We depend on speed and deception." We heard it from him over and over until his words became our thoughts. "If you boys want to stay in shape and kick the ball around, then nothing is stopping you."

One late afternoon in the second week of April, we were told to report to "the Knob"—an abandoned graveyard off Paulson Avenue in the Lincoln district of Pittsburgh, just north of Homewood toward the Allegheny River. Of course, no coaches would be present. The tenth- and eleventh-grade old guys were there—the ones who would head up the team next fall. Most of the scrubs must have been there, too.

The Knob was to be our training ground for the next few months. One of the old guys led us to it. There were no upright headstones. We slowly walked around broken glass and flat concrete markers. The ground looked stained with blood.

"Don't worry, man," said Chester. "It's just the clay, like our regular field."

"At least no oil to burn up your skin," Kendow joked.

"Still," I said, "looks like something from some horror movie, like with Vincent Price."

Our mutterings were interrupted by an old guy named Charley Harris (no relation to Teddy Harris, Mr. Clean, who was set to finish school in June). Charley Harris had just made starting guard. He stood about six-two and was blessed with a nice array of muscles under his light-tan skin. He spoke each word extremely slowly and deliberately, without any one of them missing a beat. We first thought he was acting like the gangsters in the old mafia movies: *All right, you dirty rats, up against the wall.*

We almost laughed in his face until he said, "We play real man's ball up here. No pads, no helmets, no face guards, just flesh and bones. Now you scrubs line up on defense and stop these plays if you can."

We huddled until the old guys lined up in their standard single-wing formation. Then Big George and his buddy Ron Bush lined up on the right side of our defensive line. Sonny lined up facing Charley. The rest of us formed a loose secondary line.

"Ready, set hut one, hut two!" their quarterback hollered. Before we knew it they blasted off the line, blocking our guys to the clay. Sonny stood motionless, watching us fall, then turned to see where the ball was headed. Charley reared back and punched him in the jaw.

We all heard the crunch as Sonny's jaw rippled back up into his eyes. Knocked cold, he fell without breaking his fall, blood erupting from his mouth. Everyone stopped and gasped. Laid out, mangled, I thought he was dead for sure. Practice disbanded, leaving Chester, Frankie, Skippy, and me to pick his twisted body off the ground.

"Let's get him to the hospital fast," said Frankie.

"Yeah, Pittsburgh Hospital, down on Frankstown. Ain't that far," I said hopefully.

Chester took charge. "Come on, take his legs. Skippy and I will lift him up. He ain't that heavy."

"Yeah, but it's gotta be a mile to Frankstown." Skip pointed out.

"We'll rotate," said Chester. "You two take the front."

We started to carry Sonny down out of the graveyard. He was still out cold, and we were scared to death. What if he died in our arms? Would the police think we did it?

When we finally saw the hospital a short way ahead, Skippy said, "Once we get there, drop him off at the front door and run like hell."

"That ain't right, Skip, he's one of us!" I said.

Skip shook his head. "We Negroes, he's a white boy, stupid. Huh! They'll think we did it."

"Frankie's a white man," I said. "He can tell them."

"Tell 'em what, Bronco?" said Frankie. "We can't tell 'em Charley did it. We'll get our butts kicked when word goes back to The Room.

We stopped and stood there rationalizing how we could just drop Sonny at the front door of Pittsburgh Hospital emergency until we finally went ahead and did it.

The next day rumors raced around school about what had happened, ranging from how Sonny had been attacked and killed by dogs to how a group of "brothers" had jumped him. Two more days passed with more and wilder fantasies. Ourselves, we were afraid he had died in the hospital, or maybe out on its steps.

"Hope Rabbit pulls out of this," said Kendow at our weekly scrub meeting.

On the third day, Rabbit returned to school. At lunch time, as usual, we were hiding in the boy's room, staying out of sight of the older players who would take our lunch money, make us run to get them more milk or dessert, or embarrass us in front of the best-looking girls. We were waiting there for one of the girls to bring us some cafeteria sandwiches when Kendow looked out and spotted him walking down the hall.

"Hey, boys, it's Rabbit," he announced. "He's okay and headed this way."

We waited for him, happy and relieved, until he walked into the bathroom and just stood before us. A funny-looking brace covered pretty much his entire face. He could not talk. His eyes were almost completely swollen shut. Small, purple vessels stood out from his skin. Two thin wires were looped together from his lower and upper jaw. A large pad was taped to his chin. Tears fell from his right eye as he strained to face us.

Charley had damaged him for life and there was nothing we could do about it, but Chester, Frankie, Skippy, and I felt ashamed we had simply left him on the hospital steps.

Like the rest of us, Sonny had been sworn to secrecy, and even after what had happened at the Knob, he was still a true

Bulldog, according to what we had been taught. I doubt he ever played football again, but he never did reveal what had happened. Charley was safe for now.

Weeks later Sonny's first words were, "One day I'll pay Charley back."

I don't know if he ever did.

For the next couple weeks, practice in that old graveyard was tense with resentment and rebellion as more of us fell into questioning the senseless acts of violence we were subjected to. By now my own head was full of notions about other things I wanted to do with my life.

A few days short of summer vacation, my mind was still shaken by that first trip to the Knob.

I told Skippy, "Ball at The 'House ain't what it's supposed to be."

He looked perplexed. "What do you mean, Bronco? You love ball. Next year you'll be starting right halfback."

"Naw, Skip," I said, "I like playin' but why do we got to go through all this stuff? Do you remember when we used to pick up teams at Crescent School field? Bunch of guys would just roll up sleeves and put socks in our shirts for shoulder pads and play, man."

"Yeah, Bronco, we had a good time. That Mark Prunty could toss the ball a mile and hit you with a perfect pass."

"Huh, man, and Mark ain't playing for The 'House, is he?"

"Maybe his mom won't let him play."

"Then what about that big dude Marshall Howard, man?" I said. "He was fast as they come. Coach Reno called him a big sissy in gym class last semester for not playin' football. He ain't no sissy, man. He told me that he would never play football for The 'House as long as Coach Reno is there. Some of the best players are sitting in the stands, man, and they ain't sissies either. So what gives? Man, I am seriously considering taking up boxing."

"Instead of football?"

"You heard that right."

My family was going to Boston that summer. My Dad was going to Harvard for some kind of certification in education. While we were there I thought I might ask him if he'd let me put on the gloves.

"Boxing?" Skippy shook his head.

Instead of going straight home from practice I decided to think more about my plans. My new favorite "thought spot" was at the very top of the city steps that went up the hill near our house. Sometimes the entire Homewood community seemed to be seated down at the base of these concrete stairs. Myself, after climbing some five hundred steps or so to the top, I could look out over the city. No interruptions. The summer air was warm and free of the odors people had to endure from the mills to our south. The trees were covered with blossoms. The insects were busy gathering nectar for their families. On a clear day I could see the skyscrapers miles away downtown.

My first thoughts were about The Room and how Coach Cesare controlled his players. Surely, he knew about the massive beatings we were given. Maybe he did not know how the old guys took our money, clothes, shoes, and made us do everything from cutting grass at their homes to buying them wine at the local state Liquor Control Board store. He had to know something about how poor Rabbit had got his jawbone smashed.

I remembered hearing stories about the coach before Cesare had taken over, years ago. The old coach, "Pro" Burton, had been known for hitting players in the face if they made a mistake. Reno was different. He never hit a player. The Room took care of all that. He just played with your mind, like a shrink. Maybe I *should* move on and become a boxer like Archie Moore or Sugar Ray. I tossed the idea around in my head.

What about my friends? Would they think I'd punked out? Other players had endured more than I had and had made it.

What would Dad do? I wondered.

He had played for neighboring Peabody High and Virginia State College and had made all-American football teams. I remembered the short trips we had taken across the river to the steel town of Homestead to watch baseball and visit a boxing gym. Proudly, he had introduced me to a trainer as "my number-one son" as I watched some kids duke it out in a ring.

Maybe that was his way of letting me know that boxing was what I should try. He never would tell me directly, "You should take up boxing, son." That was not his style. But those ten-o'clock Friday-night fights on TV, watching together, that was great. Just him and me. My new baby brother, Mark, had been too young. Norman, my other younger brother, spent all his time trying to figure out how to use the chemistry set I had received for Xmas. Just Dad and I laughed and joked as the white fighter was knocked to the canvas. We even split a bowl of vanilla ice cream to top the evening off. I was sure he wanted me to box.

Boston Massacres

Traveling with my father was always an adventure. He had his own method of doing everything. For one, my brothers and I were never awakened at sunrise or told to jump into his old station wagon in the middle of the afternoon. Always we were shaken from a deep sleep in the middle of the night. First he would pluck Mark out of the center of his bed and pack him neatly in the back seat. Then Norman would get one warning to put on shoes, go out, and join his little brother.

My directions were always clear: "Okay, boy, get up now and sit by the window. And sit behind me."

My main job was to carry a large glass bottle and keep the lid on tight until he signaled to pass the bottle to one or both of my younger brothers. This bottle was our mobile restroom, because Dad never stopped for anything. Since Mark was barely eight years old, I had to help him relieve himself. I hated my job. Norman had good control over his urges and usually slept the entire time. Every hour dad would check the bottle and, if necessary, slow down to let me toss the contents onto the road. Mom just sat on the passenger side up front and shook her head.

We were like the night people, afraid of daylight. Dad would drive down dark roads showing no fear of the total darkness around us. Occasionally, we would hear him softly whistle or sing small excerpts from some ancient tune.

Our Boston trip was a little different than others we had taken. Dad seldom let us see him out of control, but two weeks before we left, his patience was put to the ultimate test. It all started with a big bang on our front door.

"You Mr. Brewer?" a loud voice rang outside.

"Yes," Dad replied. "What can I do for you?" He was holding the front door halfway open. From the living room I glimpsed a short, slightly bald black man.

"I'm Harry Jenkins from up the hillside, and I want to know what your son John's going to do about supporting his baby."

"What baby?" Dad replied, fully opening the door.

Mr. Jenkins' voice rose even further as he poked a finger at Dad, claiming I had made his daughter Sandy pregnant.

Dad wasn't one to lie down to aggression.

"Okay, that's what you say, Jenkins," he countered. "I think you better calm down and get your hand away from my face."

Standing firmly, Dad was somehow managing to put Mr. Jenkins into a calmer, less threatening state. But that didn't mean that Dad was calm—not inside.

"You hear that, boy?" he said and turned as I approached. I fell into confusion as he looked me deeply in the eye.

How could she get pregnant?! I was asking myself.

It seemed to me all the guys had sex from time to time and nobody got pregnant. Somehow I thought only older girls had babies. Wasn't Sandy too young? Wasn't I too young to have been the cause? This had to be a mistake!

"It's not my baby, Dad!" I said. "But I heard she had sex with the kid next door from her—that kid named Thompson."

"Are you sure, boy?"

"Yeah, I'm sure!"

I said it loud, like I really meant it. Truth was, of course, it could have been, probably had been me, though somehow I'd been convinced back then that sex at my age had no consequences. I'd been told about what the older guys called a "rubber," that whitish thing like a rolled-up balloon with a very large opening, but I rarely had sex, and the idea of carrying something as hideous as a rubber around seemed stupid.

It was true that Sandy and I had had sex under the city steps one warm spring evening several months before. One way to look at it was that she'd trusted me—someone who seemed like a good sort of person—to know how to handle the situation, though obviously I hadn't known. But it's also true, as I recall, that Sandy had brought as much desire (maybe more) and lack of forethought to what we were getting into as I had. In any case, we'd both been willing.

"No, I don't believe he is the father," I heard Dad say in a powerful, persuasive tone. "What about that boy who lives next door?"

Eventually Jenkins stomped off the porch. And the next day he tried to run me over with his green Packard in front of the Circus Bar on Oakwood Street less than half a block from my house. I will never forget the look in his eyes as I ducked behind a power pole and his huge steel bumper bounced back with a clang.

That black iron pole had saved me for the moment, but I came away truly afraid for the first time in my life. Every place I went, green Packards rolled through my head. I was even afraid to deliver the morning paper. So when the plan came up about going to Boston for summer vacation, I secretly rejoiced, and Dad's midnight departure suited me just fine. It was certain death if that Packard caught up with me again.

The trip was longer than I expected. Normally we reached our destination by about five in the morning when everything was still dark. This time my brothers and I were awakened by the warm summer sun, somewhere in the midst of a strange new city.

"We here yet?" Norman asked.

"No!" said Dad.

"I have to go," Mark complained.

"Shut up, big ears," Norman teased him.

"Can you hold it? We almost there," said Mom.

We were definitely in Boston, Massachusetts. The streets were wide and full of cars. Horns were blowing from every direction. But Dad appeared to know exactly where we were going. After sitting in traffic, then slowly moving, we arrived at a large apartment building on Huntington Avenue, in the heart of the city.

Mom explained to us again how Dad was going to Harvard to attend some special classes. We would be here all summer.

"You kids are going to have to make the best of it. Dad has to do well...," she went on to three deaf pairs of ears.

Up in the ninth-floor apartment, Norman stuttered and complained, "I don't know anybody here. What we suppose to do?"

"Just look out here, Norman," she said, pulling back a curtain. "There's the YMCA."

Directly across the street was the largest YMCA building I had ever seen.

Dad added, "Hey, Butch, Fenway Park is just down the street. You can go to baseball games and work out at the YMCA and meet other kids while we are here."

"Yeah, Butch," said Mom. "They have plenty of stores around here. Try to get a little job. I know you hated giving up your paper route. But you can make money here and enjoy yourself, too. Mark can stay home and watch TV," she added as I slumped down in a couch, "and help me around this apartment."

She turned and embraced her youngest. Mark did not seem to mind. He was always accommodating everyone. My middle brother Norman was withdrawn and got his stimulation from reading and doing math problems.

Maybe this could work, I thought. Dad would be gone to Harvard all day. Mom and Mark would spend all day cleaning and making the meals, and Norman would sit somewhere in a corner reading his *Popular Science*. I could roam totally, hundred-percent free all day.

The next day, Monday morning, I ventured out to see what the big city of Boston had to offer. Huntington Avenue was unbroken blocks of shoe stores, restaurants, bars, novelty shops, news stands and interesting-looking people. Two blocks from our apartment was a super-wide street called Massachusetts Avenue. I heard one old guy call it the "Big M."

I started walking up the Big M and noticed a theater with the name of one of my favorite groups flashing on and off in their showcase display for that night: Isley Brothers. The ones who sang "Shout!"

Wow, I thought, *if I only had some money....*

Military guys were also checking out the sign. There were guys in white sailor suits, green Marine outfits, brown Army fatigues. In the middle of the morning, ladies were walking back and forth dressed in loud red nightclub dresses. They seemed interested in catching the eyes of the soldiers. The scene reminded me of Centre Avenue on The Hill. The music was loud and inviting and the ladies were simply hot. I knew they were probably hookers so I continued on up the Big M.

Every block was full of the same loud action. The further I walked, the drunker the soldiers looked. It was not even noon yet. This place was one big party.

"I love it here!" I chanted.

Nobody knew me. Not even Dad could extend his long arms into this wild scene to keep me in my place. There would be no Mason the cop to watch what I did and report it to Dad. I was really free to explore.

A few hours later I returned to our apartment trying to keep a straight face about all the happenings on the Big M. If I told Norman he would squeal to Mom or Dad. Mark was too young to say anything to. So I figured I would play it cool and act bored with Boston in general.

What I did not figure on was an incident my mother had experienced that day. She looked afraid when she heard me outside and opened the door to let me back in. When Dad arrived home from Harvard, she was frantic about some weirdo she kept calling the "Boston Strangler." Her face was almost white. She had just heard or read about the serial killer who was stalking people and charming his way into places. It had been in all the papers.

"I think it was him, John," she kept saying to Dad as tears rolled down her cheeks.

"Calm down, Pippy, come on, calm down, now. Tell me what happened."

He escorted her to a living room chair. Mark squeezed in beside her. We listened.

She began, "After you and Butch left, Mark and I were in the kitchen. I heard a soft knock at the front door and thought it was you or Butch coming back because you forgot something, so I went to the door. Something told me to ask who it was. So I did. A soft and gentle voice said, 'Yes, madame, I'm here to fix your stove.' I peeked out that little hole. The man seemed nice enough. He almost talked me into letting him in, but Mark pulled my arm and said, 'No, Mommie.' I don't know where Norman was.

"I became afraid and told the man to go. Mark ran back to the kitchen and came out with a butcher knife. I was so scared. We went back in the kitchen to check the back door...."

Dad tried to calm her down and convince her the man at our door had been just some mistake.

"We just moved in, Pippy!" he said. "It wasn't no Boston Strangler here."

But Mom could not be convinced. She wanted to go back to Pittsburgh. Dad conceded to her feelings enough to go right away to the hardware store and buy some door chains and a padlock for the kitchen door. He installed that home-made security system right away and calmed Mom down. That night we laughed about the incident and teased Mark about his butcher-knife defense.

I made plans to continue my tour of Boston. A day or two later, I managed to get a part-time job taking out trash for a restaurant on Huntington Avenue. It was there I met a kid named Lester.

Lester looked like a mix of Japanese and Negro. Thin and short, he stood about five-two, and his glasses looked like Coke-bottle bottoms. His hair was thick and very black, eyes slightly slanted, lips full and partly brown. He and I were the "box boys" assigned to taking out trash and crushing the empty boxes in which food had been delivered. He was somewhat of a nerd, but we became friends after two or three days.

Lester and I had plenty of time between early morning business and lunch time to talk about Boston. He seemed to know his way around the city. After work he took me on a tour of back alleys and hidden streets. We often jumped from iron fire escapes into open windows, landing in the narrow upper hallways of huge apartment buildings. The corridors were barely lit. We could hear people talking behind closed doors.

One time, we were on a fire escape when Lester suddenly whispered, "Duck down, John!"

I hunched down low. Through the window we could see some people in the hallway. Two of them were sailors. Two others were—well, they were dressed like women.

"Those girls ain't girls," Lester whispered. "It's a set-up, man."

The sailors sounded drunk. They were hugging and kissing two well-disguised men. It was kind of funny to watch. We giggled as the couples made their way down the dim hall. Suddenly four big, hairy guys with knives and small bats jumped out from behind a door. The two pretenders tossed their wigs on the floor and joined in a bloody, horrible beating.

We were scared but glued to our ringside seats.

"Come on, Les," I managed to say. "Let's get out before they see us."

"Hold up, hold up, John, just wait until it's over." He ignored my tugs on his arm. "We might get some money dropped on the floor."

"Those sailors might be dead men!"

"Naw, naw, John, be cool."

I could envision those monsters and catching and killing us.

"I'm gone, man," I said.

I hurried back the fire escape walkway to where the ladder headed down. Twice I turned back, calling Lester again to join me, but he wouldn't move.

Visions of strange men dressed in ladies' clothes dominated my thoughts as I leaped down the seven flights of iron steps to the alley, heart pounding in my head.

I began to run, but as I did I fell into some soundless spell. My body wasn't moving right. My legs were reduced to a third of the speed they should have been running. My whole life and being were trapped in slow motion. Surely, the killers would catch me now.

When I got home, my legs were like rubber, hands shaking. I could not get over the possibility that I was being followed. Even the people on that long, nine-floor elevator ride up to our apartment scared me. I fumbled with my apartment key so much that my Mom finally opened the door.

"What's wrong with you, boy?" she asked.

"Nothing, ah, nothing," I stammered, dashing into my bedroom past my brothers, safe at last, home and out of sight of that horrible scene out Mass. Ave.

Then my stomach dropped right through my pants. *Lester! What about Lester?* I thought.

I'd left him on the fire escape. Maybe he'd fled right after me, I rationalized. Or maybe he'd been killed. I kept thinking about it over and over, face covering with sweat and tears. I'd left poor Lester, who could never have defended himself against those beasts. In my haste to save my own skin, I'd abandoned a friend and broken the code of the street.

For me it was a night of knocking sounds and replays of the horrendous crime I'd seen that day. I could not sleep for thinking about what might have happened to my friend. The next morning I sprang from my bed, dressing quickly to make my way back to the restaurant.

"Where you going so early?" Mom asked as I came out of my room.

"Oh, ah, going to work."

She said, "Usually you go at nine, not six in the morning. You all right, boy? Something wrong?" she kept up the questions, always concerned about my accident proneness and ability to get in trouble. "You been to Pittsburgh Columbia Hospital so many times they ought to name a wing after you," she joked.

"Nothing wrong, I'm just in a hurry," I lied.

"Oh, okay, but be back by lunch. Dad wants to take you boys to the ballgame."

"Okay."

I dashed out the door to catch the elevator down. Minutes later I arrived at the back of the store room.

"Where's Lester?" I asked one of the short-order cooks.

"He ain't coming in today. Haven't you heard?" The cook adjusted his fluffy hat. "Lester got stabbed last night somewhere on Mass. Avenue."

I was stunned. All I could think about was that I had left him. "Oh, Lord, please don't let him die," I kept repeating to myself.

I tried to work, but everything in the little storeroom where we had worked together reminded me of Lester. It was then that I decided to become a professional boxer. I just walked off my job and walked over to the YMCA, thinking maybe if I had taken up boxing before, Lester would not now be lying somewhere wounded or dead.

Boxing was a way of life for many of the guys I saw that summer at the Y. I could feel their intensity, whether they had gloves on or not. They looked and acted confident. But my body was changing, beginning to look like theirs. Football training, push-ups, sit-ups, and miles of running had built up my legs and arms. My stomach was tightly rippled. I felt prepared to work out with the other boxers.

So I did. For two weeks I secretly trained in the Y. Every morning in the gym I would try to duplicate what the boxers were doing. I thought if I trained secretly and later demonstrated my new skills to Dad, he would surely give me permission to continue. Then one day Dad caught me hitting the speed bag.

He smiled at me and said, "So, you think you want to box, huh."

"Yeah, Dad," I bragged—loudly, "I'm ready to kick some butt."

I was surprised when he did not get angry, but reassured at this further proof that this was what he had wanted all the time. Memories came back of watching the Friday-night fights together. I also remembered going to the Pittsburgh's South Side to see the Golden Gloves competition at Market Square.

Now it all makes sense, I thought as he escorted me over to a small ring.

"Okay, let's see what you got. I will match you with that small kid over there." He motioned one of the boxers ringside. "If you beat him, I'll let you box," he added firmly. "If you lose, then give it up, son." He shifted his pipe to the right side of his mouth.

"Deal!" I shouted, pulling up my shorts.

Five minutes later, my skinny, brown-skinned opponent jumped in the ring. His trunks were too big. He could not have weighed more than 130. He reminded me of poor Lester. I looked at his long bony legs, wondering how he stood himself up in the morning.

This must be a joke, I thought as the other fighters stopped training and gathered around the ring.

Great! I could get respect from Dad and my fellow boxers at the same time. We were scheduled for only four three-minute rounds. I refused to put on head gear.

"I'm gonna knock this chump out," I declared as the audience started to cheer.

Dad stood in my corner as the bell rang for the first round. I charged out into the ring and tossed a wild right cross at his head, missed and almost fell on the floor. He seemed to vanish for an instant, then out of nowhere hit me with a barrage of punches. I regained my balance and backed up for a moment, but this little guy's gloves grew larger and larger, now hitting me anywhere he wanted. His gloves felt like stone as they hit my ribs. Over and over again I lost sight of this little guy running rings around me. Where the hell was he? The fans were beginning to laugh and shout, "Knock 'em out!"

If I only could hit him one good time, it's over! I thought as the bell sounded, ending round one.

"You all right, boy?" Dad shouted in my face.

"Yeah, yeah, I'm okay," I replied, knowing this guy completely outclassed me.

Dad put the head gear on me, and I didn't argue. But rounds two and three were pretty much the same. I never laid a hand on my opponent. He almost knocked me down three times. In the final round I fell but refused to stay down, continuing to let him show me the finer points of boxing. The fight was a total disaster. The history books talk all about the "Boston Massacre." Well, this was my own personal version, the one that brought home the valuable lesson Dad emphasized after the fight: *Never judge a book by its cover.*

After the Boston experience, in the fall of 1960, I decided to return to football. A week after we got back to Homewood, some Boston friends of my parents sent a newspaper clipping headlined, "Woman found strangled at Huntington Avenue apartment." Her ninth-floor apartment was, of course, the same one we had lived in. My mother nearly fainted.

What if that man pretending to be a repairman really had been the Boston Strangler? I wondered. *She could have been murdered. I could have been left without a mother.*

My thoughts then also took me back to Lester. Dead, maybe, and I was the cause. I had abandoned him thinking of my own safety. It seemed I was always running away. Even that summer in Boston had turned out to be nothing more than another retreat, from that green Packard and the crazy situation I had found myself involved in. It was time for me to stop running from myself and challenges I had accepted. It was time to step up and deal with whatever happened next at Westinghouse, behind that dirty gray door.

Forty-Two Towels

Few experiences in life can equal the initiation rituals that ended a player's time as a scrub on the Westinghouse High School football team: many months of total intimidation and physical and emotional abuse. No adult stood in the way of the endless demands and harassments. In fact, Coach Cesare perpetuated them as a way of controlling the team.

"Winning teams come from winning traditions," he would say at hundreds of pep rallies over the years.

Even before Cesare took over the reins as Westinghouse coach, a brutal system had been in place. As I've said, old "Pro" Burton had not minded hitting his players, or beating them down when they didn't produce. And as I said, Coach Reno never lifted a finger of his own. Instead, he carried on a player tradition of physical intimidation and punishment of other players who refused to capitulate to his will. Coach Reno controlled the minds of his players. Those who believed in this tradition played without regard to physical limitations. One-hundred-forty-pound boys transformed themselves into two-hundred-pound men with every muscle ready and willing to carry out his will or die trying.

Of any player complaining about pain, Coach Reno would sarcastically say something like, "Oh, he has a little bump on his head and he thinks he can't play." And the player would shake it off and continue to play. It was amazing. Out of The Room we came like an army of robots, displaying nothing but pure energy and force to our opponents. As our threshold for pain soared upward, so did the demands to keep us, the latest band of scrubs, in check.

There was no set future date by which you knew you would finish your time as a scrub. For some, it lasted until they quit the team. For others like me, it went on past the end of tenth-grade season, when The 'House again conquered the city. I remember the end of that 1960 season, me and my fellow scrubs sitting on the bench at the championship game at South Stadium, telling each other what had been our personal, single worst day of pain and humiliation—not that all that was completely behind us. It wasn't. The end of another championship season did not automatically lift any scrub out of the pit.

Big George got going about the late summer run we'd been sent on down the railroad tracks, beginning with the long climb up to the huge, black stone railroad trestle across Washington Boulevard overlooking the Silver Lake Drive-In theater.

"Man, I looked over the bridge from the tracks," he began. "Had to be a couple hundred feet down. And you all heard about that kid who fell from there and killed himself a few years back."

"Naw, that's just a tale the old guys told to keep us scared," said Kendow.

"Tale, my butt! It's true!"

"Okay, okay, fat boy. Is that all your story?"

"No, man," said George, "it's just the beginning. And remember how hot it was that day with our uniforms and helmets on? Man, this was August!"

"Yeah!" we agreed.

"And you had to time every step on the ties or else you just fall right through. Seemed like we were running forever and that crazy Alvin-the-Train snapping a bullwhip on our butts and singing 'Rawhide.' I thought I was going to die. Thought I was going to die," he repeated. "My legs were like rubber. I wanted to quit right then and there. And damn 'Sea Biscuit' kept pushing me and telling you guys to help me not fall, because 'Train's gonna beat you to death with his whip if you fall, fat boy!'

"And the worst part is when they let us stop and take a break. 'Who wants some nice, cold orange juice?' Moose asked and all I had was just enough energy left to say, 'Me.' I could just feel that cold, sweet juice running down my throat. Yeah, but they'd filled that carton with sand. I nearly choked to death. The 'old guys' laughed so loud nobody heard the train til it was right behind us. I almost got run over! That was my worst day."

I remembered that and other things like it. But what I remembered most was the punishment we all had feared most: the "42 towels." The old guys would often threaten us with it if anyone violated the codes and secret rules of The Room. The sentence of 42 towels meant stripping down to your underwear or jockey strap, leaning over a bench, and raising your butt in the air. Meanwhile, one of the old guys would tie a knot in the end of a towel and soak the knot in water. Then the guy would hold the towel by its other end, twirl it counterclockwise in the air and land the knot on your backside. At least, that was where he was supposed to aim, but sometimes he missed and thrashed your back.

Each other old guy would then take a turn, popping the knot on your butt. Someone always counted out loud up to the forty-second lash. The water-logged knot came down like a sledge, and the pain of each stroke was almost unbearable. Scrubs that the old guys really disliked got counted by someone who "stuttered" or "lost count" and had to restart. Halfway to 42, blood would soak the towel red. At some point, suddenly you could no longer feel your legs. If there was such a place as beyond pain, you were there. It didn't matter how many times you fell off the bench and collapsed on the cold, concrete floor. Each time, your slave masters would tell you to assume the position quickly again or they would go on swinging at you where you lay.

Late in the season of 1960, several scrubs, including myself, were sentenced to this fate for planning a scrub revolt. Day after day, we'd gone on laboring to please our masters by doing whatever they asked. Some of the old guys wanted money for lunch every day. Others stole whatever nice belongings we dared to wear or bring to school—nice clothes, expensive belts, street shoes, even down to our striped underwear. One day I wore new pointed shoes my grand- daddy had given me. Returning from practice, I saw they were gone and had to walk home barefoot. The next day, on my way to lunch, I saw them on the feet of none other than our proud team captain, Mr. Clean.

I approached and politely appealed to him to give them back before my parents found out. "Excuse me, Teddy, sir, but you have the shoes my grand dad gave me. Can I have them back, please?" I asked, but firmly.

Teddy turned, squinting, staring me right in the eye.

"These ain't your shoes, scrub, they mine," he said without cracking a smile.

I wanted to punch him in the face, but his chest stuck out gorilla-like, ready to rumble. I punked out, just shook my head, turned away, and went to lunch totally pissed off. I knew there would only be more trouble if I asked again for my shoes.

Later that week the scrubs all met over (In Pittsburghese, you could just say "over" when what you really meant was "at") Kendow's house on Maderia Street where everyone started exchanging stories about the treatment we got from the old guys. Kendow stomped his size-fourteen shoes on his mother's wooden porch.

"Damn it, I'm tired of this crap!" he said. "We should call these guys out! We got cats that can rumble with the best of them."

"Yeah! Yeah!" we all agreed.

"Let's match our boys. Bush and Big George is as big as you can get, man. And we got super big House Hardy! Who they got?"

House Hardy was the right one to mention—a tough, massive, six-foot-five kid with a giant head and a nasty attitude. As Kendow roared on, we all started thinking rebellion.

Minard tuned right into the fun, bravely taking center stage on the porch and saying, "Who they got? They got Sea Biscuit! Sea Biscuit? He's small, man. Eddie Fye-eddie? He's a playboy quarterback. He ain't gonna do nothing."

"Yeah," I said, "put House on Moose and we all can jump Willie Hancock, Larry Malone, and Fields."

"Whoa," said Slaughter. "The one we got to worry about is that crazy-ass Train."

Big George nodded. "He's crazy strong, man, and he can't feel pain. Anyway, maybe we should wait til dress-up day and hurt them on the field during practice."

Dress-up day was Thursday. The varsity wore their game dress at practice, and no physical contact was made. Since Friday was game day, the old guys were careful not to get their game uniforms dirty. George figured that would put them in a mood not to expect an attack. Besides, they'd be so busy trying to get their pictures taken by the school photographer and local fans, they wouldn't be ready to defend themselves. Kind of crazy, but that's what George came up with, and it sounded okay to most of us there.

Then Kendow said, "Naw, man, let's just walk into that imaginary circle next week and start kicking butts. We become old guys overnight and put an end to this madness."

We all began to rethink our approach, arguing for the next two hours, shouting and screaming until Kendow's mother asked us to leave. Finally, though, we decided to revolt the following Tuesday after our weekly scrimmage. We figured the old guys would be too tired and too surprised to defend themselves.

Kendow said he would spread the word to the other scrubs who weren't at the meeting. A few days later, someone leaked this information. Chester, Kendow, and I were blamed for the plot. That was the time of my greatest fear, knowing I would have to return and face the punishment. I remember the three of us standing at one end of The Room, holding our breath as Moose pulled a fresh white towel from a stack that Little Pete had left on one of the benches.

"Here's one!" he shouted and tossed it to Mr. Clean. Teddy looked sinister, calm, and deeply composed. He never smiled or displayed his emotion. Now, he just stood there, dark eyes penetrating our souls. His voice was barely audible, his movement slow and deliberate. His look of disgust told us plainly we were going to get the beating of our lives.

How could this be? I wondered as we watched two other old guys take turns tightening an incredibly large knot. *And where's Coach Reno now?* He had to come inside, if only for a second, to give us one of those pep talks. Chester and I both stood there, one eye fixed on the door, the other on the old guys adding water and tightening the knot. We knew we were trapped, doomed, and afraid we could not endure what was about to happen.

"All right, drop 'em, scrubs," Moose ordered. We unfastened our football pants and let them drop to the floor. "Turn around and stick your scrub butts out!" he hollered. "Count 'em with me, punks!"

"One!"

Two other old guys lined up with knotted towels of their own to hit me, Slaughter, and Kendow at the same time. The first blow hit me in the middle of my bare back.

"Two!"

We gripped the wooden bench. Teddy hit Slaughter so hard I could hear his bones crack.

"Three!"

The third one caught me at the top of my cheeks. My neck snapped forward. I blew out a blast of air as though I might blow out the pain. Beside me, Kendow seemed to take the pain pretty well, but Chester's mouth was quivering.

"Four!" we all shouted.

The trio of old guys were perfectly timed.

"Five!"

Only Kendow and I responded. By now the knots were stained with our blood.

"Six!"

Moose was swinging wildly now, hitting me on the back of my neck. When I reached back impulsively to see if my head was still attached to my neck, he went crazy, swinging at my face and landing square on the bone of my left cheek. Quickly I lowered my head. All the old guys were laughing now and cheering Moose to continue.

Kendow stood straight up and dodged the next incoming towel. He had never been beaten this way, and I could tell how mad he'd become. For a moment I thought he was ready to go berserk. He had that strange look. All of the players jumped up that instant awaiting Kendow's next move. He turned to look at the other scrubs, seated on other benches. I think he expected they all would jump in and challenge our tormentors. But one by one they lowered their heads. I knew now we were truly doomed. From then on, the beating picked up the pace. We lost track of the count. I went dizzy and fell to the concrete. Kendow and Chester were beaten down to it.

A few of the senior players were motioning for the beatings to stop. One or two hollered "42!" "I said 42, damn it!"

The count went dead as we lay there limp on that cold dirty floor, tears cascading over our cheeks. The old guys left. Our fellow scrubs helped us to stand up and dress.

Our journey home was slow and painful. We were more or less carried for two blocks to the playground at Belmar School. Kendow cussed the others out for not helping us fight the old guys. Chester and I were too hurt to complain.

Big George offered to buy some pop at the corner store. Skippy walked beside me, holding me up and several times picking me off the ground. Our clothes were so badly soaked with blood that a woman offered to call an ambulance.

"No thank you, lady, we got things under control," Minard waved as we walked by her house. Further on as we stopped again for a breather, he shouted, "Okay, who squealed?!"

"Don't know, man," Kendow replied. "It sure in the hell wasn't me."

"Man, that was sure some beating you all took," Skippy sympathized. "Let's see how bad, Brew." He peeled my jersey up my back. "Damn, Brew. You might have to go see a doctor. You got some deep cuts, man."

"Can't do that, man," I said. "Remember what happen to Rabbit? Pittsburgh Hospital called his parents. If my dad finds out, my football days are over." I was rambling now, about how I would manage to sneak in the house without my parents knowing I was hurt.

We drank the pop Big George had brought back from the store and continued up Frankstown Avenue. We stopped at Hale Street, dropping Chester off at home. Then Kendow, Skippy and I walked slowly up the hill to Oakwood where they helped me up the steps, around the side of the house, and planted me at the back door.

Dad and Mom were in the living room, at the front of the house, engrossed in the news on TV. I snuck in, crawled upstairs to my bedroom and quietly shut the door.

Norman and Mark, who shared the bedroom next to mine, saw me pass their door. With the shake of a fist, I motioned them both not to say anything. Alone in my room, I looked down at my bloody sweat pants. The backs of my pant legs were tight. It was going to be painful taking them off.

Maybe I should just climb in bed and let them dry off, I thought, then realized they might be even tighter when they dried. *No, better take 'em off.*

Very slowly I started to peel them off. A sharp pain almost made me cry out. This was not going to be easy. Then I remembered the old cowboy movies and how they would bite down on a rag to muffle their cry as the doctor dug out a bullet. I bit down on something and started to strip, screaming and crying in silence. Damn, it hurt so bad. My entire backside was badly cut. Nevertheless, I was home free. Ten minutes later the throbbing had slowed down enough for me to lower myself carefully onto the bed and cover my nakedness with the sheet. After a short while I slid into sleep.

A few hours passed as I lay there sleeping on my stomach, my soul submerged in a warm, comforting dream in which there was no Room. My body had healed and I was running free in a field of yellow flowers. Pretty girls ran beside me, brimming with smiles and inviting notions.

"AHHHHHHH!" A blood-curdling scream awoke me to my mother standing over me, wailing, hands pressed against her narrow face, eyes spitting out tears. I thought something terrible must have happened to her. She looked so shocked. My father came running in his underwear.

"What's wrong, Pippy?"

"Look, at him, John!"

I looked around and was surprised to see the sheet was covered with blood that had run down onto the hardwood floor.

"What happen to you, boy?" Dad demanded.

"What?" I blurted.

"Somebody stab you? You get shot?" Mom rattled off the questions so fast I could not collect words to reply.

As usual, Dad was cooler than Mom. He escorted her out of the room and returned to examine me. I made up every story I could conjure on the spot. Anything but the truth might get him off my back. I settled on the explanation that I'd cut myself jumping over a wire fence.

He removed the sheet from my backside and said, "Boy, you think I'm stupid! I work with kids every day. I know the difference between a cut from a fence and a lash. Did you get this beating from the football team at Westinghouse?"

"No, Dad, I swear I cut myself," I kept repeating.

He looked me in the eye and said, "Okay, boy, I better not see this again. Can't you see how upset your mother is?"

I nodded. He went out and started running water in the tub, then collected the bottle of disinfectant from the medicine cabinet in the hall and poured that also in the tub. After a while he called me in, saying, "Get in, boy, and soak yourself before those sores get infected."

He'd had medical training and I trusted his advice totally when it came to healing any wound. What I did not guess was the pain I would feel as I lowered myself into that tub of disinfectant. My screams were louder than my mother's had been. Still, Dad was letting this lie ride. I know he knew how I had got the beating of my life. He knew about "42."

What it meant to me right then was that I had passed the ultimate test. Soon, I would be a varsity Bulldog for Westinghouse High. Despite all the pain, I was proud of becoming what I thought was a man.

"Golden Gloves"

November 1960, my tenth grade year: the last brown leaves had fallen from the many oaks around our neighborhood and now lay drenched in yards and gutters. The hours of daylight had dwindled down, spooked away by Halloween pumpkins, and football season was over. Our dreams of becoming regular players were right around the corner. The old guys had managed to beat every public high school team in the city. We were city champs once again. I had even got to play in the last quarter of the championship game after the first team ran up the score. After the game, my dad reminded me about the fifteen-yard penalty I had caused.

"I saw you throw that elbow at the Allegheny player, boy!" he laughed. "Keep your elbows attached to your body, Butch."

"Yeah, Dad," I replied. "I know."

We all were so excited after the game that not one scrub complained about the goodies we had to supply to the old guys. Skippy and Chester and I had to buy Mr. Clean a bottle of Ten-High whiskey. Moose wanted a bottle of Thunderbird wine. Fortunately for us, our street buddy, Delrico Reed, looked old enough to buy liquor at the state store on Oakwood. He simply donned his gray, blocked felt hat and pranced inside. Nobody ever questioned his age. In fact, nobody ever *knew* his age. Delrico had left school young because of seizures. He knew every corner of Homewood and The Hill. Sometimes he spoke "pig Latin" to loosen up the tension.

"And-over-hay the ooze-bay," He joked that evening, reaching for the Ten-High.

"Naw, man," Kendow told him, "we can't share that. It don't belong to us. Meet us over Leo's house and we'll give you first hit off some other poison." (Leo Loar was another one of us scrubs.)

We turned over the booze to the old guys and reassembled with more of our buddies in the underpass outside The Room. We were still excited about winning the big game. We were even more excited that our scrubbing days would be over.

"They turn us now, right?" Big George said with a smile.

"Because they won it, right?" I asked Frank McCellan, another Bulldog scrub I'd been friends with since Crescent School days. He was also a top academic student and always seemed to know the details of things when I myself was clueless.

"Wait," said Ron Bush, Big George's best buddy, who had also made it with us through those first two seasons. "First, we got to go through GG."

"GG, GG, what's GG?" I asked.

Everyone just stopped and stared at me.

"Frank," I said, "what's GG?"

Frank smiled his all-knowing smile and said, "GG is 'golden gloves,' Brew. It's the last thing you do before you go completely over. They match you up with your buddy and you have to fight until someone goes down or until the old guys are satisfied."

"Yeah, man," said Minard. "You got to fight to the end or you could get another 42 towels!"

We pondered this new twist as we walked down Murtland toward Frankstown Avenue.

"Damn it, more crap we got to go through." Disgustedly, Big George tossed away an empty juice container. "Who do I got to fight?"

"Probably your main man Ronnie—or big House Hardy," Kendow laughed.

"House? House? That monster, man?" George mumbled.

We all fell out laughing.

"I don't want to fight my best friend, either, man," he continued.

"Hey, that's the tradition. You may have to fight Ronnie, man," said Chester.

"Who you going to fight, Slaughter?" George asked.

"I don't know, man," Chester replied. "Probably little Minard."

"No big challenge for you," George said.

I thought about who was *my* best buddy. Maybe me and Chester; we were very close. Both of us played right halfback and we walked to school together. But Chester was not as heavy as me. The very thought of fighting my best buddy made me sick. I felt even sicker thinking about taking another 42 towels. I decided to forget about it as well as I could for the rest of that championship weekend. Three-o-five Monday afternoon, when school let out and GG came down, was coming all too fast, but meanwhile we had two days to party.

Of course, all the cheap wine, girls, and song we had that weekend did nothing but slow us down on Monday at three-o-five. And each and every one of us was afraid of failing this one last test. I still felt disappointed in myself for leaving little Lester, and other commitments I felt I'd run away from most of my life.

That afternoon we entered The Room with uncertainty written all over us. We sat on the long bench, sizing up whoever we thought we were going to fight. There were no more "doughboys" in The Room. Two seasons of intense conditioning and physical challenge had transformed every player on the team. We were all pumped up with hard, lean bodies, necks, backs and legs strong and fully muscled. And of course we'd grown taller. Even Minard had grown two inches in a year. Big George had slimmed down, large and hard. Coach Reno's Room had done a good job turning out a new hard, ruthless flock. We could run faster, longer, and harder than most kids our age. We'd been taught to suck up pain like cherry cough drops. And Coach Reno's endless control over our minds had elevated our performance well beyond the breaking points of our young bones.

And now was our "graduation day" into varsity. There we sat as the old guys walked in— no coaches or trainers. They looked our way with huge, expectant grins. Then they caught our attention with clapping and chants.

"Bulldogs! Westinghouse Bulldogs!" they yelled, beating time with their hands. "GG! GG! GG!"

They pointed at each of us, one by one. Then the door slammed shut and Mr. Clean walked slowly into "the circle." The shouting stopped. All I could hear was my own heart beating.

"It's time for GG," he began in a calm voice. "Listen up! When I call two names, you enter the circle and battle until I say to stop. If you dog it, then you will get 42 towels. Ron Bush and George Harris: you first."

The two big friends stood up and faced off. They started to circle each other, pushing out punches that barely touched. Big George hurled a soft right jab which Bush blocked and countered with a soft jab of his own. For two minutes they danced around sniffing loudly in and out.

"Stop, punks!" Moose hollered. "Look like you two made this fight up at the bakery last night. If you don't start to fight for real you'll both get 42."

Now Bush became a raging bull, forgetting friendship, and smashed Big George in the face. George responded just as wildly and the fight was on full blast. They knocked over benches as the old guys cheered and jumped up and down. Even we scrubs were allowed to cheer for our favorite. For fifteen minutes they kept slugging each other until Big George lay bleeding on the floor.

"Okay, boys, that's what we want to see here." Teddy clapped. "Okay, next, Brewer and Larry Berry."

Someone in the rear said, "Brewer is called 'Bronco' and Berry they call 'Block.'"

They laughed as we entered the circle. I was a little surprised they had picked Block. I thought maybe they didn't know that Chester Slaughter was my soul mate. Larry the Block was short and extremely muscular. Even his nose had muscles. But he was also a proper-speaking gentleman, not at all street. I knew he would try to fight fair, no surprises; I knew the advantage was mine.

No way I wanted any part of 42 towels. Right off, I sucker-punched him hard on his hard head and set out to beat every square knot off his body. He was very strong but totally unprepared for a street-style fight. We rolled around on the floor until we seemed to please the old guys and Teddy told me to stop. I got up, still completely pumped.

Minutes later Teddy called out the two names we had all been thinking about since the old guys had called for Golden Gloves.

"Dave Young! House Hardy!"

Every player moved forward to catch this big battle. The rumors said Dave was a tough guy who had spent two years at Thornhill correctional institute. He stood about five-ten, with a huge chest and strong arms, and was known as a big-time brawler. Likewise, big "House" was known to hurt people year around.

This was excitement. Dave rushed House Hardy and jacked him up, lifting all 280 pounds of him off the concrete floor. At 180 pounds himself, Dave held House in mid-air, then slammed him down hard. We all were amazed Dave could pick up and slam House Hardy.

"Wow! Did you see that, Bronco?" Minard screamed.

I said, "Yeah, bad dude, all right!"

Dave landed on top of House, pinning him and tossing punches into House's head, chest and face. House grabbed Dave's hands and managed to tie him up for several minutes. The fight became a wrestling match with House on the bottom. They finally stopped the bout, declaring Dave the winner.

The matches continued for another hour and a half. By eight in the evening we were on our way home. We were now fully transformed players. Now we were "old guy" Westinghouse Bulldogs.

Reflections on Train

Winter found us still licking our wounds from the 1960 football season. I often daydreamed about it in class, replaying dozens of conflicts and the beatings we had endured, in and out, all season long. My mind seemed dedicated to comprehending why we had been so abused over and over. But we scrubs were not the only ones who had been sacrificed that season.

I also thought about Alvin "Train" Allsberry and his own extreme sacrifice in the course of the championship game. One week before it, he had been working under his father's truck when some gasoline spilled on his chest. A spark ignited it, burning him from chest to ankles.

News about this horrible accident quickly spread around school. Everyone—especially the scrubs—feared our star running back would not be able to play.

"Damn, if Train don't play, we gonna lose," Minard worried after the Monday practice.

"Yeah, I know, man," Kendow added. "And if we lose, then they ain't gonna let us turn to be old guys." He tossed his helmet at the bench.

"This entire year will be shot!" said Skippy.

We all sat down a while, then dejectedly changed back into our streets. Coach Reno had left practice early to visit Train in the hospital, but by the time we were dressed and ready to leave, he'd returned. We sat back down and waited—old guys and scrubs. The Room was quiet. Even the odors seemed to diminish.

Coach entered the circle. We all hunched forward to hear every word. He turned his head to meet each pair of eyes, like a Roman emperor staring us down. When he spoke it was very controlled.

"Alvin Allsberry got burned a little, but he will be with us on Friday."

The Room went crazy. We clapped and, over and over, chanted Alvin's name. The old guys high-fived each other, and all of us thanked Jesus for giving us hope once again. Reno motioned us to stop. His eyes glazed over.

"He's not a cry baby like some of you girls," he joked. "Alvin understands that he would be letting his team down by running home to his mama. Remember, your mothers will be watching you Friday! Your community will be watching you Friday! We have a tradition around here of winning and if you want to be part of that tradition, one little burn or twisted ankle or bump on your knee won't stop you!"

By the end of his speech he was barking. Once again, the players went wild. We screamed and shouted, "Westinghouse forever!" and embraced each other like never before, pumped back up by our coach's news.

Four afternoons later, the day of the game, Train entered The Room with a blank look on his face. He acted like nothing at all had happened, but a large white pad protruded out the top of his checkered shirt. He said nothing, only grunted and winced as the trainer helped him remove his clothes. The burns were still fresh. I could smell them. Most of the players quickly went out to board the bus that would carry us over to South High stadium. A few of us remained. At first just happy to see him, now we watched, shocked, as the trainer and assistant coach stuck large pads on his chest and back, covering his burns, then wrapped him with several rolls of gauze. By the time they were done, they had wrapped up most of Alvin's body. At the end of an hour, his uniform was finally on.

Alvin Allsberry played the entire game, bringing yet another championship to the famous coach of the Westinghouse Bulldogs.

When we got back after the game, once again Train braced himself for ultimate pain, then roared as the trainers attempted to remove the bandages caked with blood. It was a sight I will never forget, his skin coming off with the blood-soaked gauze. Nor will I ever forget his screams.

Even his tears inflicted more torture, more grief. They had to clean the wounds before they could wrap him again with fresh gauze. Uselessly, they tried to ease it by spreading Vasoline over the burns. Surely, I thought, they would return him to the hospital. But as far as I know, then or now, he didn't get back into hospital care until his grandmother got him back in.

That was sacrifice.

"Hey, Brewer, get your head out of the clouds," Mr. Dino, my print shop teacher, woke me from my dream. "Fix the speed on that," he said, pointing to the back of the press.

But years move on, and the new one, 1961 would be my year to stand tall. Inside, I drifted back to my own heroic vision, seeing myself in that blue-and-gold championship jacket with "Bronco" embroidered on the chest. But I had to buckle down, Dad was saying, get back on the books and maintain the C average that would keep me eligible to play.

At the same time, with winter almost here, my popularity with the girls seemed about to take flight. Parties were everywhere. Kendow, Vann McCellan ("Little Mac" we called him, not to confuse him with Frank McCellan), Chester, and I would start with the rowhouses on Hamilton Avenue. We could walk slowly down Hamilton listening for music. Most of the time our old buddy Delrico had already scouted out the hot spots, where the girls were. They had dime socials in those houses every week. Usually we did not have to pay if we knew someone inside. Seldom did these parties have food. We always seemed to end up in a darkened basement guessing who was a girl and who was a boy. If you didn't watch yourself, some "hard leg" might become your dancing partner. The wrong selection could start off the fight—with you in the middle—ending the party.

Our local YMCA was better. We could at least see who we were dancing with. And we could come out in the open, now that we were "old guys." We even went to high-class dances at Holy Cross Church on Kelly Street, where the girls were rich and pretty.

Every weekend we jumped from party to party. Two girls we knew were very popular because of the nice "house parties" they gave. Cynthia Wilcox's house was near Baxter School. Her basement was always decorated with red, blue, and green lights. Most of the time, she even had food. Margo Goodson lived in a new house on Coal Street in Wilkinsburg, a town on the edge of the city, bordering Homewood. Her basement was called a "game room." Their parties were a step up from the rowhouse parties. They were sexy, well-kept girls who liked ball players. An invitation from them meant you were getting popular, too.

My life seemed to be under control until one Saturday night when, after the usual ritual of trying to complete my weekly chores, I dashed down to a dance at the old Bennett Street School.

All of my close boys were standing on the steps waiting for me to arrive. We had to make our big entrance together as one mean, cool team. We strolled across the large wooden dance floor and posted ourselves along the wall, checking out the babes. Chester and Kendow slid away to ask some girls to dance. Skippy and I stayed behind, still comparing notes on the best-looking of the bunch.

Bright red caught my eye at the entrance. The girl in the dress was butterscotch brown, shapely, with large, dazzling eyes. Her smile extended from cheek to cheek. Her lipstick perfectly matched her dress. She stopped directly in front of me, batting her lashes. I stood there speechless, completely under her spell.

"My name is Mary Lou, baby. What is yours?" she asked softly.

I babbled something like my name. Before I knew it we were dancing to Bobby Freeman's "Do You Wanna Dance?" and went on dancing after that one, whether the record was slow or fast. She laughed as I stumbled over my two left feet. I did not care that I had blown my cool completely, one-hundred percent. Her wonderful smell and soft skin excited every part of me. Suddenly her brother Earl was motioning for her to leave. The dance was almost over. I followed her out and asked her number.

"Why sure, honey child, it's Churchill 1, 5, 4, 6, 5."

I repeated the number twenty times in my head and watched her walk down Bennett with Earl.

Afterward, my boys rushed up behind me shouting and chanting, "Bronco's in love!"

"'Call me, sugar daddy,'" Kendow teased.

Skippy slapped my head, saying, "Huh! Snap out of it, man, you looked like a fool!"

"Yeah, that girl got deep into your nose, boy!" Kendow poked me in the chest.

How foolish I felt. I had lost my cool. I had broken every rule the older guys had laid down to me last year, hanging out on the city steps. I could just hear the La Rells, the doo-wop group that had come out of Homewood and was opening for some famous acts, advising me how to keep the upper hand on women. Somehow Mary Lou Brown had confused me.

In reality, despite my football reputation and despite my misadventure with Sandy, despite the fact that I joked and played a lot of games around them, I was really somewhat shy around girls. Other guys I knew were far more sexually engaged. They loafed with an older crowd who smoked, drank and attended truly wild parties. We called them "Hey babes" because that's what they said, passing time on the corner of Frankstown and Homewood, hollering as the girls walked by heading home from school.

But with Mary Lou, I'd got that same out-of-control feeling that had shamed me so much back in grade school. Much as I mistrusted how she seemed to lift me out of my "tuff guy" self, I definitely enjoyed the special attention she gave me after that dance. I simply could not believe how romantic I became as soon as we'd crossed paths.

But how could I face the guys at school? I could hear them laughing and teasing me again during practice when they found out Mary Lou liked to hold hands and kiss in public. That was not the way the cool cats of Homewood handled romance. If you were cool, after a dance or party a chick would simply be there for you to walk her home in the dark, and everyone understood you were only "going together"—not married or caught in a flaming relationship. But I wasn't sure I was quite that cool.

For a month we saw each other almost every day. One Sunday she wanted to go to a movie in East Liberty at the Sheridan Square Theater. We rode the Frankstown trolley over there late in the afternoon. After the show we decided to walk back to Homewood. Before long we were at Westinghouse, down in the tunnel, near the entrance that led to The Room, and we started to kiss and explore.

"Stay right where you are!" From behind a bright light, a middle-aged white man appeared and flashed a badge. "Security!"

"We ain't doing nothing!" Mary Lou shouted.

Didn't matter. He ordered us over to a station wagon where a lady was sitting up front.

"Get in back!" he ordered.

I couldn't tell if he was armed, but the lady stepped out and the two of them pretty much forced us into the rear seat. A heavy wire screen separated us from the front. I tried to stay calm, telling these security people how innocent we were. But nothing I or Mary Lou could say could stop them from hauling us away.

There's something about Mary Lou that I may know more clearly now than I knew at that moment years ago. I must have known then that both her parents were from the Deep South. Both chewed tobacco and spat in a can. Did I also know that they and their Mary Lou came from a line of people called the "Geechee," famous for their powers to curse?

Suddenly Mary Lou stopped crying and froze like she'd just been zapped with a ray-gun. Her face turned red. Her big eyes fixed on the neck of the man at the wheel in front.

"*I curse you to die, die, die, die, die...,*" she said in a voice I had never heard.

Sensing an energy beyond my comprehension, I slid away, pressing myself against the door. Up front, the white lady told her to shut up. But Mary Lou didn't shut up. The lady kept saying stop, and I tried also to calm her down, but she continued to curse the driver until we arrived at juvenile court in the Oakland district of Pittsburgh, a few miles away.

The couple took us upstairs and down a narrow hallway. Four tall, gray, metal cylinder tanks stood upright at the end of the hall—like the helium tanks balloon men used to blow up balloons for a party, or like the submarine torpedoes I'd seen in flicks about World War II. How weird it was to see them in the juvenile court detention center.

"Don't touch them tanks!" the man ordered.

They escorted us into a vacant room and made us sit on a bench near the window, then left, closing the door behind them. Then the lady returned and asked our names and telephone numbers. Mary Lou wouldn't respond. I tried to explain once again how we had simply cut through the school grounds on our way home. Somewhere in this process, the lady revealed that she and George, the man, were married. Together they were employed by the school board, patrolling the property of the district.

Suddenly something crashed in the hall. Then someone shouted, "Hey, you okay?!"

The lady dashed out to see what had happened, and we looked out behind her. The tanks had toppled. Nearby, her husband George lay on the floor, apparenty knocked out cold. More people appeared in the hallway. A short while later, I peeked out and saw paramedics kneeling over George, trying to revive him. His wife was frantic. Ten minutes later we all knew they'd failed.

"He's dead," said someone.

I turned to look back at Mary Lou. She smiled, relaxed like nothing had happened. We went back to the bench and sat in silence a while until someone came in and said my father was coming to take us home.

The next day at school, people were saying Mary Lou had killed some white guy. The rumor was running so strong that my science teacher, Mr. Ray, pulled me aside between classes, asking what I knew.

Between me and Mary Lou, after that night, things were a little different. We still talked and claimed each other as boyfriend and girlfriend, but—at least for me—in a less serious way. And when she was seriously on my mind, my way to clear her out was to run. So in something like the way Lester had been part of what had led me into boxing, Mary Lou was a big part of why, in the spring of 1961, I decided to go out for Westinghouse track.

That season of running started for me after meeting Dad's friend, Mr. Clarence Doaks, the Westinghouse track team coach. Mr. Doaks was the perfect athlete. During his own career as a runner, he had been a world-class hurdler and had missed going to the Olympics by one small tenth of a second. He was a tall, aristocratic-looking black man, often mistaken for a lawyer, doctor, or movie star. Mr. Doaks took a personal interest in developing his team. He really understood how to get the best out of us all. The winter of 1961 he had encouraged me and other football players, like Orin Richburg and Leo Loar, to join our schoolmate Jimmy Allen, a dedicated hundred-yard sprinter, running indoor track at Pitt's field house. There we ran against college sprinters and high school stars. Gradually that spring, other guys on the football squad also went out for Westinghouse track.

Our training and conditioning covered more than wind sprints, 400-yard dashes, and walking on our toes. Quietly, skillfully, Mr. Doaks taught us about thinking independently. He helped us free our minds from the tyranny of The Room. We were encouraged to respect and enjoy sports with a positive outlook. My father's words and ideas on sportsmanship flowed from Mr. Doaks. He helped us gain perspective on winning and the price others might want us to pay.

He told me, "If you get hurt, you need to watch out because you are young and your bones are still forming. Anyone who cares about you will not let you continue to damage yourself. There's always another day to play the game."

Coach Doaks was new at The 'House—not an established legend like Coach Cesare. He was the first and only Negro high school coach I ever saw, before or during my high school years. He wouldn't openly criticize Coach Cesare or his methods, yet whenever he expressed his concerns about how we were developing as young people, I heard what they implied about Cesare and the general order of Westinghouse football. Doaks spent a lot of time talking to us about our future plans and how we were doing academically.

I don't mean Coach Cesare wasn't concerned if one of his key players was about to fail a subject and lose his eligibility for football. He was concerned, but he handled things a little differently. He was known to have private words with the teachers about his players. One way or another, we were all protected from the more ambitious, "no-nonsense" teachers, as if our way had been neatly paved before we ever arrived at Westinghouse.

"Bronco, we got it made," my friend Skippy would always say. "Just go with the flow. Don't buck the system."

But I knew something was wrong. I knew playing ball for the champion Bulldogs was indeed an honor, but I also knew my math skills were not very sharp, however they had seemed back in fifth grade. When Coach Cesare offered to talk to my teacher and Mr. Doaks offered to help me with my math comprehension, I understood more about them both. Not surprisingly, we heard rumors that Coach Cesare hated Doaks' guts.

Two weeks into the track season, every football player who ran track got a sample of Reno's wrath.

"I see you track boys walking around the school on your toes, like some kind of ballerinas, instead of planting your feet firmly on the ground like a man," he barked in one of our closed-door meetings.

The other players laughed and pointed at Orin, Leo, me, Minard, and the other guys who had gone out for track. We might be "old guys," but Coach Cesare was putting us on the spot as trouble makers as well. Coach classified players like us as friends with my old mentor, Clyde Hefflin, who had also played for Westinghouse but had fallen into Reno's bad books. It was a toss-up as to which one he hated more: Doaks or Hefflin. But our minds were clear: despite his fire and damnation speeches we were going to run track *and* play football.

The Price of Running

We spent the early summer days running the streets of Pittsburgh in search of an open basketball court, an empty football field, or a track to test our speed. Coach Doaks arranged for me and Orin Richburg to compete in a meet at Kennywood Amusement Park. We were surprised to learn Kennywood even had a track.

Kennywood Park still sits today on a bluff overlooking the Monongahela River, across from Braddock, an old steel town on the edge of Pittsburgh. Its black cinder track was on the far end of the park. It was known to us that Kennywood did not let Negroes swim in its all-white pool, and we were a little apprehensive about attending this meet. But we trusted Coach Doaks with our lives, and once we arrived and warmed up, all our fears faded.

The track was narrow, just six lanes for the hundred-yard dash. In the far lane, Orin and I noticed a short, stocky, dark-skinned kid. Moments later we got down for the start, the gun sounded and we were off. Halfway down the track Orin and I were in the front when suddenly that kid in the far lane flew by, winning by at least four yards.

"Who in the hell was that?"

The officials seemed as amazed as we were. They kept checking their watches until one of them announced a winning time of 8.9 seconds.

"That's a world record, isn't it!" Orin declared.

In fact it wasn't, because the track was not only narrow but a few yards shy of a full hundred yards. Even so, we all knew the young brother who had just blown us way was special. Years later we found out his name: Bob Hayes. He'd gone on to be crowned as fastest man in the world at the 1964 Summer Olympics.

Word quickly got back that we had ignored Coach Reno's warnings not to dare go out for track. On our first day of football practice that August, he stomped onto the field with the blue practice vests that would go to his first-string offense. He looked pissed off, eyes shifting back and forth. Without hesitation, he tossed one to Spider Webb at fullback. He flipped another to Hindu Henderson at quarterback. More slowly, he handed Melvin Myricks, who had also run track, a vest to play left halfback. I moved closer to the front. He stared me in the eye and squinted, then tossed the final backfield (right halfback) vest to Chester Slaughter.

As far as I was concerned, that right halfback spot belonged to me. I smiled and joined the defensive squad as middle linebacker.

"Middle linebacker?" said Skippy as we huddled on the field. "Bronco, you are fast as any offensive back."

"Naw, naw," I said. "Man, I want to do some hitting. I plan to disrupt every play until I get back my position."

"Okay, man," he said. "Hope you know what you doing."

We scrimmaged for forty-five minutes. Then Reno blew the whistle and reluctantly instructed Chester to hand his blue vest over to me.

"Brewer, put that on!" he ordered.

I walked over and proudly put on the vest. Coach's eyes were burning the back of my helmet, but the position was mine. To myself I proclaimed a first victory against The Room and Reno's control.

Our pre-season games were against teams outside Pittsburgh in a suburban and small-town league called WPIAL (pronounced "WHIPPY-ull"). We only had two weeks to prepare for the first, against Aliquippa High School. Two days before the game, Reno attacked any notion that any player could "buck the system."

"We may have some traitors among us," he announced. "Watch who you associate with. You know, of course, that damn bum Hefflin, hanging out at Schenley, trying to get them to start a 'room.' I say he is a bum. He was a bum when he played for us years ago and he is a bum now!" he shouted. "Trouble makers will divide the power of The 'House, don't you see?"

The truth was, Clyde Hefflin wasn't just "hanging out" at Schenley. He wasn't a paid city coach, but he had official permission to be part of Schenley's coaching staff. We sat there, no one speaking back. But after practice that same day, walking home, we talked.

"I don't know about you guys," said Kendow, "but I think Reno is jealous of Clyde. What you think, Bronco?"

I said, "Hey, Kenny, Clyde taught me half of what I know about football and my dad and uncle taught me the rest."

"Me, too!" said Minard.

"I'll never talk against Clyde," I said and curled my fist.

"Check it out, man," said Skippy, stopping to take center stage.

Skip seldom aired his views, though we were all familiar with his grunts and groans whenever we met amongst ourselves.

"What has Reno taught us about football?" he asked. "We only have four plays to learn. Huh! We run our plays from the oldest formation in the country."

"Yeah, I know it, Skip," Minard agreed. "We run the single wing. Single wing, man, don't nobody in the damn country run the single wing but us!"

He was basically right. All of the teams we were playing used the T-formation or some version of the wishbone offense. Single wing was from back in the old, old days when Jim Thorpe was playing ball. If all you learned in high school football was the single wing, what use would you be to a college team?

"Reno thinks we are too dumb to run any other kind of offense," said Kendow. "We never pass the ball, man. We got Hindu, one of the best passers in the city, and they use him for a blocking back. Spider, our fullback, handles the ball. What kind of stuff is that?" He went through the motions of throwing a pass.

"It's always been that way," said Chester. "Hindu's whole family produced quarterbacks who could throw and run the plays. But Coach Reno, he got this style from Coach Burton, twenty years ago. Burton never used guys like Hindu. Never mind passing. Just run, run, run!"

The WPIAL league was something else, compared with the rest of the teams in the city. If you know professional football, you've heard the names of some great pro players who have come out of those Western Pennsylvania hills, and the list does not begin or end with Joe Montana. In those rich suburbs or small, tough steel towns along the rivers—Aliquippa, Clairton, Monessen—it seemed like the world existed for football, and the schools had practice fields, lighted stadiums, big flashy bands, and, most of all, all kinds of coaches and equipment and actual grass on the Friday-night field. Out there, fall Friday nights were reserved for the bright lights of high school football. Our city league played afternoon games because the city fields had no lights.

It was another world out there, and of the city teams, The 'House was about the only one that could often stand up to those guys.

We battled Aliquippa down to the gun and ended the game in an 0-6 loss. In the week after that game, Reno continued to drill us about "outside interests" dividing the players. I don't know what he meant to do by that, if not cut some of us off from the team fanatics. Some guys still worshipped the ground he walked on. Each day, I could feel the tension rise between us in The Room. More and more often the fanatics were accusing starters like Bootsey, Rudy Dean and me of lacking loyalty to the team. In reaction, we bonded amongst ourselves, isolated from the rest.

Two days before our second pre-season game, against the Mt. Lebanon High Blue Devils, Rudy, who played center, came up to me and said, "Bronco, man, I know some of our guys ain't protecting you as much as they should." He was telling me certain other players who were supposed to be blocking on my runs were hearing from someone higher up they didn't really need to work so hard on my behalf. "That's Reno's doing," he added, loud and clear.

Rudy had always been somewhat of an outcast himself. He was a senior but quiet most of the time. I never remembered him harassing us or making us do him favors. My instinct was to trust him.

"What are you saying, man?" I asked.

He put his right hand on my shoulder and said, "I'm saying I will protect you, man. After I center the ball I'll be with you all the way down the field. Anybody in your way I'll take out, man."

I thanked him and studied his middle-weight frame. He was slightly taller than me, but he weighed just over 170, ten pounds less than I did. I wondered if he was really big enough for the job. The big guys were our tackles, Bush, Big George and, of course, House Hardy. They would have blocked for me, but I was always in motion before the ball was snapped. By the time our big guys could pull to block, I was gone. That left me with the possible protection of our two pulling guards, Larry Berry and Frank Bisceglia, but they were like Rudy—smaller than me.

Oftentimes, I had no protection beyond the deceptiveness of the handoff from Spider, our fullback, the primary ball handler in a single wing. If the defense lost sight of the ball for an instant, I could be well into their secondary before they knew I had it. Then how far I got toward the end zone depended on downfield blocking, which Rudy was saying he'd give.

Even within WPIAL, Mt. Lebanon was not your average opponent. The Blue Devils were a top-rated team from one of Pittsburgh's richer southern suburbs. The outcome of our game with them had no bearing on our city league standings, but that didn't matter to our coach, who reminded us about our loss to the Devils last season. He badly wanted revenge for that loss, and we had to want it as bad as he did.

As the sun went down that evening, our yellow, worn-down school bus rolled into Mt. Lebanon's parking lot, and one by one our guys stepped off, suited and ready to play. We'd all noticed the vast array of sports cars there as we'd rolled in. I focused on a red Stingray with its ragtop down. The driver was a cute, white Blue Devil cheerleader girl. Three others like her jumped out and made their way toward us, smiling and pointing at us guys like they'd known us for years.

Bootsey moved to the head of our pack. "Look, man," he hollered toward the field. "No oil, no humps, tonight we play on pure green grass!"

One of the cheerleaders laughed. "That's our practice field silly," she said and pointed off toward a stadium down below the school. "That's our game field. That's the one that grows on sod."

She giggled and rejoined her friends, running down toward the stadium gates. For a long moment we stood feeling stupid, staring down at an even more beautiful field. We could not believe our eyes. Whenever we played out at places like this, it was like discovering the eighth or ninth wonder of the world. Thousands of people were filling the stands. Someone threw a switch and the night lights ignited. In the stands, a large band in blue and white blared out a song. Everywhere were signs saying "GO DEVILS GO."

This was going to be some kind of game. Somehow, all of my concerns about Coach Reno, The Room, even whether I'd eaten all the spinach Popeye said I should, disappeared. Once I walked onto Mt. Lebanon's field, the cheering faded out of my hearing. I no longer saw the Blue Devil signs. My old identity slipped away. Whoever I had become was intent only on destroying any obstacle between us and victory. I wanted those Blue Devils worse than our coach. I could feel my mind and body bonding together on that.

Once the game was under way, I thought I was going mad. I could not feel pain, exhaustion, or remorse for landing blow after blow to the heads, backs or mid-sections of my opponents. I had never before this game experienced so much rage, focus and sheer energy. On defense I felt invincible. As though hypnotized, play after play I lined up just behind big House Hardy over center and plunged into any and all attempts to block me, trap me, or run the ball around me.

Offensively, I shouldered the weight with our other backs, all making progress up and down the field. Many times Mt. Lebanon's team was confused by our speed and deception. As for their own offensive drives, their spearhead was an extremely fast running back we quickly labeled "Snake," number 12. Several times we managed to stop and contain him on runs down close to the goal, but finally he scored.

"We got to score, Bronco," said Hindu Henderson, once we had possession again, pointing at me in the huddle. We were somewhere around our own 30-yard-line. "Okay, 45 on two."

Rudy Dean turned to me and nodded. Seconds later I went in motion from right to left and took the handoff from Spider Webb. I cut sharp into a hole near left end and started down field. I could see Rudy's number 66 crossing the field to protect me.

Suddenly someone shouted, "Get that yellow nigger."

The words exploded in my ears. Not believing what I had heard, I slowed down, turning back toward whoever had called me that. I almost stopped to hunt him down.

Rudy came up and pushed me forward. "Go, Bronco go! Keep movin'!"

I snapped back to reality and dashed to the end zone 70 yards away.

Five minutes later we celebrated again in the Blue Devils' end zone after I intercepted and ran the ball back 33 yards.

Time ran out on the Blue and White: final score 12 to 6. We had beaten one of the best-trained, best-equipped teams in Western Pennsylvania.

News of our upset spread like wildfire around the city. The Saturday Pittsburgh sports sections reported the game in detail. That following week at school everyone was all smiles and stories.

"Man, did you see all them rich white folk out there?" said Kendow as we strolled the halls.

"Huh! Huh!" big Skip answered. "And they must have had ninety guys on their team."

Minard said, "Man, they had a whole gang of trainers and ten assistants helping their team."

"Yeah, then here we come in a broken-down old bus, one trainer, two coaches and forty-five players." Big George laughed. He passed me an orange juice and grinned when I took it and found it was empty.

Chester said, "We still won, boys. No matter how many you have, there's only eleven guys on the field at a time."

"That's true," said Bootsey, "but they still got all the advantages. That stadium was beautiful. The women were beautiful. Sports cars and all."

"I agree, man," said Kendow. "Seems like they got it easy, all right. But rich or not, we beat their butts."

When our regular city league games started, opponent after opponent simply fell down the moment we walked onto the field. We were crushing team after team. Most of the time our first team played only the first two quarters. By the third, scores of 30-0 were common. We never ended with an odd number of points because we never even practiced kicking extra points. Coach Reno didn't believe in working for one lousy point. We just kept running those same four plays until the other side dropped.

Everyone said we could clinch the city league title easy as long as we beat one good last team in our division. That was the Schenley Spartans, which drew its players from The Hill. The Spartans were, of course, being helped by my mentor Clyde Hefflin, himself a former Bulldog.

By that time, assistant coach Dennis had left The 'House to become head coach at South Hills High. The new assistant coach, Jeff Wilson, spent a lot of his time scouting upcoming opponents. Reno used his reports to tailor our plays to the weakness of the opposing team. More often than not, Jeff's reports were about specific players who were strong performers, weak links, or hotheads with predictable behavior.

"They have a big line," Jeff told us, "also blazingly fast running backs, but no passing game at all. Francis Peay is their big lineman. Three running backs aren't big but, like I said, they are really fast. Ron Porter runs to his left around end. Bailey runs to the right, and a fullback named Banks up the middle. I heard a rumor they got a secret weapon named Brown who plans to pick a fight with Henderson, and get him tossed out the game."

Reno waited for Jeff to finish and said, "They got that damn spy, Hefflin, don't they, Jeff. I knew it would come down to this game against him. Christ sake! He has got half our players following him. I don't like it at all. The other half act like them 'Hey babes' from Schenley."

Jeff said, "Well, we can take them if we don't let their Porter and Bailey turn the corners."

"Yeah, but what about scoring on them?" Reno asked.

"Run Brewer around left end and Myricks hard on their right side. Peay can't be everywhere."

Later, supposedly out of our hearing, their discussion continued. Reno seemed to agree with Jeff, adding that he wanted to turn big House Hardy loose on them as he had at Mt Lebanon, not "confusing" Hardy with a lot of formations and trick defensive plays. Just break the line, and keep their speed backs from turning the corners. For Reno it was a critical game. As he said he saw it, if Schenley beat The 'House, the Bulldogs' champ tradition would decline. He wasn't about to let that damn Hefflin destroy all he had worked for. What he and Jeff had to do was impress on their players how important it was to stay true blue to Westinghouse.

That practice week before our bout with Schenley, Reno brought us all in for one session after another. He cussed and spat out speech after speech about Hefflin stealing our tradition, our Room, and selling out to the kids from Schenley. We felt like we were playing against Hefflin, not the actual Schenley players. Reno's display wound us up and killed off any inclination to mention anything that Clyde had done for us at any time in our lives, or even that we'd ever crossed paths.

The team captains made sure we also denied having friends on the opposing squad. I disagreed, but silently. My association with kids from The Hill had started long before I had entered Westinghouse Junior High. As I have said, my father had taught in The Hill. I had fond memories of the many trips I had taken all over there with and without him. One of my best friends, Ron Porter, was from The Hill. Ron and I had competed at just about everything, running track, playing hoops at the Centre Avenue YMCA, even comparing notes on Hill or Homewood girls we tried to seduce.

Ron and I talked on the phone for hours during the week before the "big game," bragging and laughing at each other. I knew he would call the night before the game and talk big stuff. We tried our best at laying head games on each other. He'd say, "We gonna beat your ass, man," and I would call him by his nickname saying, "You're gonna *kiss* our ass, Beans, not beat it." We laughed and shouted until our mothers reclaimed the phones.

Seeing his name circled as our enemy on the display board in The Room did not sit right with me. I was equally uncomfortable with anyone portraying Clyde Hefflin as Mr. Evil. I still had a mind of my own that Reno did not control.

I knew Coach Cesare would try over and over again to weed out players like me that he saw becoming too much like Hefflin. Reno preyed on his players. Clyde represented all the things Reno could not control. He was strong, independent and aware of the game.

But the talk about Clyde's starting a "room" at Schenley was a smokescreen, a rumor, spread to enrage Reno. And it worked, at least in doing that.

Friday afternoon home games in Homewood always excited everyone. Our entire school attended. Teachers cheered louder than students. People came from all over the city. Our bleachers, the nearby hillside, and even the overlooking Lincoln Avenue Bridge were filled with Bulldog fans. Some of the fans gained entrance to our field by walking through the Silver Lake Drive-In theater. They would bring food and plenty to drink. It was like a black cabaret. They all came home to The 'House.

Our battle with the Schenley Spartans was indeed a test. They were everything Coach Jeff had described at the briefing. We battled our way up and down the field for three-and-one-half quarters trying to hold them off. They came within inches of breaking more than a dozen plays. Ron Porter and John Bailey each nearly broke into the clear for them several times. We had to gang-tackle their fullback and wrestle him to the oily field. From all around, the sounds of shoulder pads clashing, helmets colliding and grunts from both teams filled the air.

In the fourth quarter, finally, Melvin Myricks scored and gave us a 6-0 lead. On our next drive, Spider carried up the middle with great determination. He played like Jim Brown, ramming his small, hard body time after time into a mass of arms, backs and chests. But that drive ended. Then Schenley scored, finally, after so many attempts. Then we countered again, regaining the lead at twelve points to six.

The game ended in exhaustion. We had survived against an opponent as prepared as we were. Somehow, the mystique of The 'House had carried us through to the final gun.

Back at The 'House that evening we slowly re-entered The Room, each player deep in his own thoughts about the game. I knew the Schenley High team of 1961 was slightly better than we were. Their only problem was that they did not know it.

In the weeks after that, we faced and beat less formidable opponents. I often ran to my left with few if any blockers. Reno designed a new play for me he called "3-wide," which was like a naked reverse, a run without blockers. He said it was meant to fake out the left side of our opponents' line and depended on my superior speed for outrunning the defense. He didn't mention anything about anyone's desire to control me or get me hurt, but it wasn't hard for me understand what all was really going on.

Sometimes 3-wide worked. Often it did not. It was not easy to run, and I never knew what to expect. As many as six defensive players might know the play was coming. All I could do was prepare to ram my head into whatever wall awaited me. Sometimes I broke tackles and bounced off elbows slammed at my head. Frequently, I returned to the huddle dazed and counting the stars. At that point in my life, had I ever even heard the word *concussion*? But Reno seemed to love that play, and the fans loved to see me break tackles and make yardage the hard way.

By the end of our season, after winning our division and then the championship against Langley High, I was rewarded with the city writers' all-city Most Valuable Player award. I also received a second, ongoing prize in the form of a series of blackouts that had begun during regular season play and landed me, right after the fnal game, at St. John's Hospital on Pittsburgh's North Side, out of my mind.

The Awakening

Two days after the Langley game, I regained some consciousness of my surroundings. Plastic I.V. tubes were taped to both my arms. My nostrils were jammed with more tubes. White linen sheets wrapped tightly over me from the waist on down. I felt like a muscle-less hotdog stapled in a big white bun.

I panicked.

"I can't feel my legs!" I shouted.

No one seemed to hear. Again I screamed. Still not a soul.But someone would have to check on me soon, wouldn't they? I hoped.

Perhaps this was not a regular kind of hospital at all. The smell here was different from my old hang-out, Columbia Hospital where I'd been for previous treatments, or Pittsburgh Hospital where we had taken Rabbit. Those hospitals were always noisy with nurses and doctors running around and cut-up patients all over the place. This place was extremely quiet and, apart from me, apparently empty.

Is this place a madhouse? I thought. *Have I gone insane?* I could hardly remember what had brought me here, nor much of anything else.

Mid-Novembers always ran short of daylight. Through a large window I watched how gray and dull the city was becoming just before Thanksgiving. I began to weep and long for the freedom I had before landing in this wretched place.

"Good Morning!" said a soft, slightly female voice. "I'm Harold. I'm here, little boy, to take care of you."

Harold was not a girl, but I was happy to see anyone at that point, even a weirdo.

"Morning," I answered reluctantly. "I'm not a little boy. I play football for Westinghouse High Bulldogs."

"Oh yes, I see. Well you certainly are a big one, aren't you," He said, leaning over me to adjust my pillow.

"What the hell you doing?!" I raised both arms to block his hands.

"I have to change your sheets and pillow case," he said. "You have been out cold for two days now. They gave you a spinal and I know you can't move."

"Spinal?! Spinal?! What the hell is that?" I raised my voice and held up the sheet for protection. "Get the hell out of here!"

Before I knew it, three nurses and a doctor rushed in, barely hesitating before the nurse stuck a needle in my arm. My rage faded into a black hole.

I awoke sometime after noon the next day. There was a stillness in the room. Through nearly closed, thick window curtains, sunlight streaked my bed. My arms were still hooked up to the tubes.

But I was not upset any more. The white sheets wrapped around my body smelled fresh, clean, and were no longer tight, though I still could not move or feel my lower parts. I also could not hear myself speak.

Perhaps I'm dead, I thought.

"Do you believe?" a voice whispered. I followed the sound to the sunlight.

A tall, black man was standing near the opening of the curtains. He must have been over six-foot, dressed in black and wearing a top hat. He approached my bedside with a look that was pleasant and wise. He smiled, extended two large, brown hands, and placed them on my forehead. A warm, divine power poured from his hands.

"Do you believe, John?" he asked again.

"Yes, yes, yes," I answered, happy to hear my own voice.

My body began to shake and move up and down. The power caused me to rise up, pulling at the plastic I.V. Moments later two nurses dashed in, upset to see me on my feet on the bed, hunched over, popping out my tubes.

"John! How did you...?" one nurse said, as the second nurse eased me back down.

"Where is the man in black?" I asked. I felt so relieved and happy to have been uplifted by his power.

"What man in black, child? Ain't nobody been in here!" the second nurse declared.

"Yeah? You had to see him, he was standing right here." I pointed where he'd stood.

"I said nobody been in here, boy. You crazy! I been on duty all morning. You pulled out your I.V., boy, and the alarm went off."

She continued to try to convince me.

The tall black man had disappeared into the daylight, but his power had brought back my voice, and I could move now for the first time since I entered the hospital.

"You been daydreamin', child," both nurses kept insisting as they laughed and handed me a cup of water. "You been asleep."

Were they right? All I knew for sure was that now, suddenly, I was truly awake for the first time in my seventeen years. Until the visit from the tall black man who I knew was real, my world had been one of great illusion. Childhood stories I used to make up about UFO's landing near our house... my obsession with "superheroes" and great sports stars...my constant running everywhere I went...my lack of self-control over natural bodily urges...my quest for an identity as an athlete to win the acceptance and approval of my peers.

Why else would I ever have gotten invited to those parties? I could hear them saying, *You know who that is? That is John Brewer, the football player.* Being a Bulldog had opened those doors and made me what I thought was cool, what I thought was a man.

I had endured great pain and permitted Coach Reno and his Room to abuse me just to gain membership into that exclusive club called "Bulldog football." The other players may have had other reasons to endure The Room, but I suspected theirs were similar. Yet we also all knew deep down inside that "tradition" did not really care if we played fractured, concussed, or covered with burns. It didn't care whether we might go to college. Most of us never did move on to play college ball, much less to the pro's.

"Tradition" only wanted to keep winning those championships year after year. The day we graduated or otherwise left the school, we would no longer be the positive, contributing forces behind the "winning tradition" Coach Reno preached about. As far as that was concerned, our lives were over. In fact, ex-Westinghouse ball players often lined Homewood's Frankstown Avenue near Willy's International Pool Hall. It was a sad sight, watching these ex-players simulating single-wing plays with an empty bottle of wine.

It was time for a change.

Transfer

By Christmas, winter was in full bloom, blanketing our steps with clean, crisp layers of white.

As kids we'd found plenty to do when it snowed. Little John and I would hustle, shoveling snow for old people afraid of falling. Kendow would organize a small party of kids taking turns tossing rock-filled snowballs at the trolley poles that stuck up from the tops of the streetcars to the power lines above. Once that steel pole was knocked off the line, Sparks flew like the Fourth of July and the car would simply stop. We all got a big laugh out of seeing the conductor dash out, waving his fist at us as we stood ready to beat it, up the city steps. Billy Evans, my neighbor, loved to go sledding. He loved the excitement and danger of riding down Tokay Street near Crescent School.

I still loved to kick the snow piles off the curb into the street, but this Christmas of 1961 my childhood days were over and, now that I was back from the hospital, my father and I were going to talk about my future. He had been promoted to a higher position at the board of education's main office in Oakland, across from the big green campus of Pitt.

One evening he called me into the dining room and asked me to sit. Our dining room meetings were always over something serious, and that's how he looked that night.

"Listen boy, we have been looking at tapes from the football games you played this year, and I don't like what I see."

"What do you mean, Dad? I had a good year."

"No, it's not about how many touchdowns you made or tackles you missed. I saw you running without any protection and that damn Coach Cesare doing absolutely nothing."

"Yeah, well, you might be right."

"By the time you got to the Allderdice game you hardly knew which way you were running. Do you even remember running the wrong way, boy?"

"No, ah, not really, Dad." I tried hard to recall.

"Well, you did. And now you've just got out of the hospital for what happened last game of the season. You were having concussions in your brain, and Reno just stood there and watched you almost die. I'm not letting that happen, son."

I leaned forward to hear the verdict.

"The way I see it," he continued, "I have two options. Number one," he hesitated, "I will close football down for five seasons at Westinghouse High."

I gasped. I had no doubt he could do that through his power down at the board. He stared at my blank and silent face, then opened up on how much he knew, which was plenty—right on the case and full of facts. He knew about The Room, Coach Reno's "unusual" methods of control, and why I had ended up in the hospital not just last November but also earlier on the team for a troubling shortness of breath. He told me that other parents had complained about the hazing, with horrible stories concerning their sons.

"Son," he said, "we been working to stop this kind of terror, but we have not been able to prove it until now. Also, this coach is not preparing his players to go on to college."

I sat glued to my chair, sure now that Dad and my track coach had been talking.

He said, "So few ball players from Westinghouse even make it to college, yet every summer Reno Cesare conducts football clinics at places like Michigan State. He uses you kids to fill his own pockets with loot. Did you know he's out on the speaking circuit making jokes about his big stupid players who can only run four plays? Did you know that?"

I cleared my throat, tried to gather my thoughts. One part of me wanted to stand up and shout, "Amen, Dad, shut 'em down!" But another part stayed stuck in that chair, loyal to my friends on the team. No football at The 'House for five years? I did not want my friends to suffer that because of Reno. And I knew Dad was serious about making a change.

I also recalled again what seemed to happen to the best guys on the team, over the years. Most of them never went anywhere in football after high school. They simply joined that gang of ex-players on the block. The more I thought about it, the madder I became.

"You're right, Dad," I said. "But it's not fair to the other guys to close it down. Some of those guys live for football. If they can't play they would simply die."

Dad stood up and replied, "By next year we are going to change the board's rules concerning school attendance. It's something called open enrollment, and the board has already approved it. Students will be allowed to select any school they want and not be obliged to attend a certain school based on where they live. This will end Reno's control of kids in Homewood—at least his power of selection. Unfortunately, the new rule will not take effect until after you graduate."

He sat again, shuffled some papers from a tan folder, and said, "I had to go out and get a loan to pay your hospital bills." He showed me a letter to an insurance company in Chicago that had handled my injury. "But at least new students who want to play ball will not have to be subjected to what you've gone through."

My thoughts shifted back to Marshall Howard, another student at Westinghouse High who had never gone out for the team. I remembered how Reno criticized him for not playing ball. Reno had even called him a "sissy" in front of his friends, because Marshall would have been one heck of an end, a first-team selection without a doubt. He was over six-foot-two, extremely fast and built like a locomotive. But Marshall's folks were not about to let him play under our abusive system. Besides Marshall, I had played sandlot ball with dozens of other kids who were better than some of our first- and second-team guys.

"What's the second option?" I asked.

"The second option is I transfer you over to Peabody High School in January. But as for more football, those concussions still have not healed. If the doctor says you can't play next fall, that's it. If he approves you to play by then, I will consider letting you play."

By now he was reading my mind. "As for revenge, son, well, things will work out the natural way: only the Lord will decide."

One early January morning in 1962 I climbed aboard an 88 trolley headed for Peabody High. Geographically, it was Westinghouse's closest athletic rival, its district separated from ours mainly by the ravine where Washington Boulevard runs from Homewood down a mile or two to the Allegheny River. Around that time, the Peabody side was mainly white, the Westinghouse side heavily black. The school itself was on North Highland Avenue, beyond East Liberty's business district. The streetcar was full of older people going to work. Steel mill workers, older ladies carrying shopping bags, and small children sat by the trolley windows. We all watched Homewood disappear as we headed down Frankstown Avenue. Before long we were rattling down Penn Avenue in the heart of East Liberty's stores.

"Highland Avenue," yelled the conductor.

Slowly I stood and wrapped a hand around a post near the center doors.

This is it, I thought as the doors folded open. The school was four or five blocks from the stop. My new challenge was minutes away.

I reached Margaretta, the side street where the huge building began, and turned down toward the school's main entrance. It looked ancient, like some Roman builder had gone mad. Massive pillars stood at the top of a long, wide flight of stone steps that stopped at the heavy main doors. Students were running up and down the steps. Some had book bags on their backs—not something you'd see too often back at Westinghouse. Others were just strolling along with each other. The scene was different from The 'House. The atmosphere was so relaxed, I thought it wasn't a high school at all. Everyone looked so happy-go-lucky, *Is this some kind of nut-house?* I wondered.

Inside it was not Westinghouse, either, where you walked down the hallways—loud and intense—looking as tough as you could. Not the Westinghouse halls where only the strong could roam. I walked toward a door marked "Office," fixing my eyes on other students as they passed. Both girls and boys were smiling at me. A few even said a respectful "Good morning." Maybe they were treating me nice because of my football reputation. Perhaps they had heard about my transfer and wanted me to feel at home. They probably figured I could help their Highlanders win a city title for the first time since 1953—the last time any city team had taken the crown from The 'House.

Yeah, that's got to be it.

Then a high-pitched voice said, "You must be the new kid from Westinghouse. John Brewer's your name, right?" The boy was short, neatly dressed, and white. "I'm Steve. We have the same home room with Mr. Z, upstairs. If you like I'll show you where it's at. Mr. Z will give you your schedule, okay?"

"Yeah, thanks, man, nice of you to offer. I don't know where anything is around here."

I followed him up.

"So, how did you know my name, Steve?" I began to drill him. "Guess you heard about my leaving Westinghouse, huh?"

Steve stopped and said, "Yes, the principal's office told me to watch out for you."

"Guess you want to know why I left after playing for a championship team," I continued.

"No, not really, John. I didn't know you played sports. I tried out for baseball last year, but I didn't make the team." He laughed and adjusted his brown-frame glasses. "What sport did you play?"

I was surprised. Steve could care less that I had played football for the Bulldogs. I could sense that he selected friends based on who he liked. His bid for friendship was refreshing and different than I had experienced before.

He introduced me to my homeroom teacher, Mr. Zurosky, who, like everyone else, called himself "Mr. Z". He invited me to take a seat while he called the roll. I listened to the last names of my homeroom class. There were Jewish kids, Polish kids, Italians, Irish, and one lone Negro—me. This was going to be an interesting school. They all joked and laughed *at and with* each other. Kids who were smart were called "nerds." Italian kids were teased about the mafia. Polish kids were called stupid. Irish students were accused of drinking and beating up smaller white kids. Jewish kids were accused of hiding money inside their long noses. Since I was the only Negro in the class, nobody joked openly about Negroes. Instead, I was invited to laugh at everyone else. I could barely contain my laughter as the steady storm of joking swirled around the room.

I did wonder where the other Negroes were. I would see them here and there in the halls and in some of my classes. Finally, after three weeks of enjoying this new kind of peace, I bumped into "coon's corner."

"Hey, soul brother, look here," someone shouted at me as I walked down a corridor toward my next class. My eyes must have been playing tricks on me. I thought some white kid was talking like a brother and calling me out.

"Hey, my man," he said, "I'm Earl Woodyard. You know, Barbara's brother."

Earl looked like a Jewish kid, in well-pressed khaki pants, a light-blue, button-down shirt, with a yellow knit sweater wrapped around his neck. Mid-winter, he had on expensive-looking penny loafers with no socks. His skin was almost white. He kept flipping his long brown hair back from his forehead. I moved in closer.

"Oh yeah, right, Earl, Barbara's younger brother from Jack and Jill," I answered coolly.

Now I had a frame of reference. Jack and Jill was the ultimate Negro upper-class youth group in Pittsburgh and some other cities. It was sponsored by their mothers, and for me to be any part of it my mother had had to be accepted into their group. All of the fathers were professionals, like Dad. When Mom had got me into it, I had been expected to improve my social skills and learn better manners, but I'd disappointed her in that regard. Nevertheless, I did recall Earl and his pretty sister, Barbara.

"So, Earl, where are the brothers and sisters, man? Where do they hang out, man?" I asked.

"Right here, man. This is 'coon's corner.' Just wait five minutes and they'll be here."

I looked around and saw nothing but a wall of brick and a window facing toward Highland Avenue.

"Naw, man, I mean where do you party at?" I said.

The way I saw things, If you lived in Homewood, you partied there. If you lived in Garfield—or in Shadyside where Earl and Barbara lived—I guessed you partied there.

Earl spoke slowly but properly. He said, "I go all around and party. Last week we all went up to Stanton Heights to some Jewish kid's house."

"Who did you dance with? Any sisters there?"

"No man, just Jewish chicks and a few Italians."

"You were dancing with white girls?! Come on, man, you lying to me." I tapped his yellow sweater.

"No, man, brothers party with white girls all the time."

I fell back against the wall trying to remember when I had ever even touched a white girl. Of course, there was that time at Highland Park swimming pool, years back. That one touch had almost got Billy Evans, Gus and me put in jail. And here we had Earl Woodyard and other brothers doing everything! This school was really something crazy.

"You gonna play for Peabody this year?" he asked.

"I don't know, man. I'll probably run track this spring and see what the doctor thinks in the fall."

"Say, if you don't mind me asking, why did you leave the Bulldogs? You guys been city champs every year. I hear you were some kind of star. Why leave a good thing?"

These new questions made me uncomfortable. I did not want to talk with him about the reasons I had transferred. I changed the subject to a cute, light-tan girl who had just walked by.

"Who's she?"

"That's Carol Ball. Forget it man, she goes with some guy in the service."

"So?" I stuck out my chest.

"Ask Big John or James, man. Here they come—" he broke off and tip-toed away.

The trio of brothers walking toward us must have scared him off. They walked up to me and we shook hands.

"I'm Pres Robinson from Garfield, man. This is my ace boon coon, James."

James Boyd smiled at their relationship and turned to slap hands with his buddy.

I knew the third brother already: Johnny Yandell, who lived, of all places, on Murtland, right down the street from Westinghouse. John's Dad, Henry Yandell, was a life-long friend of my dad and a football mentor to most of the kids in our 'hood. Johnny's parents had somehow avoided sending John to Westinghouse and had got him into Peabody instead.

John stood about six-three, and was also blessed with good looks and a quick, sharp tongue. He was constantly making jokes, though his wit was sometimes hard to figure out. Sometimes I could not tell if he was insulting someone or making a compliment. Johnny was a natural-born athlete and comedian, all in one big package. He played every sport around, as well as a mean game of chess.

To my surprise, John never pressured me to play football at Peabody. Instead, he simply became my best friend. Every day we met at coon's corner to talk about our childhoods and, gradually, about our hidden ambitions as well. We even began to talk about working together to rally Peabody's football team to defeat Coach Reno Cesare.

As winter turned to spring, I began to feel like my old self. I wanted to get back to football. I wanted to get back in shape and prepare myself for the upcoming season. After several months of inactivity, I was weighing over, 215, out of shape, but determined to shake off the fat. That, not any Mary Lou, was one reason I went out for Peabody track and, by end of the season, had lost over 16 pounds. By end of spring I felt stronger than ever before and ready to ask Dad about playing "Highlander" football that fall. But I waited for weeks for the moment to ask. I knew Mom would not support me, and every time I managed to gather enough nerve to ask, something happened to dampen my courage—like her sharing another letter about the hospital bills they were still paying off.

Feeling guilty, I kept backing off until Johnny Yandell gave me some interesting history. Like my dad, Henry Yandell had attended Peabody back in the Depression. Apparently, he and Dad had played football for Peabody together, whipping Westinghouse pretty good. And other players on Peabody's 1962 team also had fathers who'd played for Peabody back in those days, and under the same old coach who was still running the Highlander squad.

Some kind of omen? I wondered. I confronted Dad with my new rationale. Even he had to be impressed with this astonishing discovery.

I pleaded my case for an hour. He listened closely, but in the end he would not say I had his permission. He did suggest I prepare myself for a series of tests to monitor my condition, and scheduled me to visit Allegheny General Hospital on the North Side in two weeks. He also wanted me to visit Doctor Young, one of Dad's medical friends. From what I could figure out, Doctor Young was a psychiatrist—a "head doctor" fully equipped with the soft voice and the long leather couch. I became a little nervous just thinking about opening my mind to some head-shrinker. But if I wanted to play football, Dad assured me I had to talk to the shrink.

Week after week I played a mental tug-of-war with Doctor Young until one day he broke down the barrier. Silence has its own power, and Doctor Young was a master at using silence to make you want to speak. He would just stare into your mind without uttering one word. Once he was inside, everything you thought was hidden became 100% exposed. Like a woman in the supermarket, he just strolled down the aisle of your mind and selected whatever he wanted you to see there in your brain. Before I knew it, we were talking about my childhood, anger, sexual frustrations, and need for revenge.

By August of 1962 I began to understand things about myself I had never realized, including the tremendous damage done to both my mind and body in The Room. Just as the late summer practice began, Dad signed the slip that would let me play football again .

My tests at Allegheny General were over. So were the sessions with Doctor Young. It was time to hit the gridiron with all of my strength and speed. To *my* mind, this was going to be a season people would talk about for years.

Dad wanted certain precautions to be taken before I re-entered the game. He and I met with Peabody's head coach, Richard Meyers. Coach Meyers was a short, wiry old man, clean-shaven with white wrinkled skin. He was in good shape for his age. In looks he reminded me of Harry S. Truman, who'd been President when I was younger. Coach's speech was fast and high.

I noticed a large, dark red, globe-like object sitting on his desk.

He handed it to me saying, "This special padded helmet is for you, John."

"Uh...."

"Try it on, boy," Dad insisted.

I placed it on my head and removed it in disgust.

"I'm hearing weird noises inside," I protested.

"You will get used to that soon, John," Coach Meyers replied, smiling and handing the helmet to Dad.

Dad was clear: "This is your protection, boy. You need to wear it. Also, I asked Coach Meyers to let you work your way into the running back position only as the season progresses."

"But I can play halfback or fullback now," I said.

"No, Butch, you will take too many blows to the head. Besides, you like playing middle linebacker, don't you?"

I hesitated, then nodded agreement, and we all shook hands.

For the first time since last November I ran out onto a football field, this one stretching along Highland Avenue at the far end of the school. It had no more grass on it than the one I'd left behind, but its version of red dog was a slight improvement over the oily, concrete ground at The 'House.

I changed my number to 70, in honor of my defensive all-time professional hero, Sam Huff of the New York Giants. Like me, Huff played middle linebacker. He was known as a fierce competitor who smashed running backs into the ground. He was one of the few men who could single-handedly bring down the great Jim Brown. I practiced hard for two weeks to prepare for our first pre-season game.

That first game for the Highlanders was a painful eye-opener for me. The bus was scheduled to leave our school at 6:00 p.m. on an early September Friday night. When I arrived at 6:15, the bus had left already. Coach Meyers had told us to be there at 6:00, but why hadn't he made them wait just fifteen minutes so I could have been there to do my part?!

"They don't play around," I said to no one but myself. Even Dad had warned me that Coach Meyers did not put up with any stuff. Old, white-haired Dick Meyers had been Dad's and Uncle James' coach back in the thirties. Back then as now, he was the total opposite of Coach Reno Cesare, always seeming more interested in helping correct our characters than he was in winning games. Now I had no one to blame but myself.

The Duel

Peabody versus Westinghouse: a running duel that fall of 1962.

September days were always welcome after the back-burning August heat. Grass or dirt, every football field on God's earth was blessed with a steady stream of cooler air. Nothing was so rewarding as that cool, simple breeze.

We worked on all facets of the game. Coach even spent time on practicing field goals and extra point kicks.

As a team, we started to bond despite our differences. Still, our roll call sounded like the United Nations:

"Robinson, Kappernaros, Phillips, Maiello, Zortea, Levey, Brewer, Richey, Gentile, Telakis, Yandell, DeRigga, Gay, Bisceglia, Norcik, Henderson, Carrabba, Iacurci,..." Coach hollered them out.

The "Iacurci" was Danny, who had been with me trying out for the Bulldogs until he got fed up with the insults and hazing on a day that Train had ordered him down on his hands and knees, and not to get up until he'd found "an Italian ant."

We ran from a T-formation. Pres Robinson and Vernon Phillips were the halfbacks, both fast and elusive. Mike Telakis, our fullback, was slow and not very powerful, and I felt destined for his slot. However, I knew Coach Meyers would not let me run the ball yet despite the pressure that other players were putting on him to let me carry.

We played together as a team and started to win every game. Playing ball for Peabody High, unlike my stay at The

'House, was fun. By mid-season in October, we and Westinghouse both remained undefeated and were headed for a showdown.

Community people were beginning to talk about our upcoming battle. Corner stores and barber shops were bursting over with predictions. I could hardly show my face at the Friday YMCA dances. My "honey child," my still less-than-completely-serious girlfriend (so I thought), Mary Lou, and her friends teased me about how little chance we had against the unbeatable 'House. My next-door neighbor winked as I returned home from practice one day. Everyone was giving me the countdown, like I didn't know the big game was Friday at the Westinghouse field.

My Bulldog buddies managed to ignore me that entire week. I could just hear Coach Reno screaming in their ears, "Brewer's a traitor, a damn traitor! You must crush Peabody. Remember, your family will be watching, your community will be watching. Hell, all of Pittsburgh will be watching this game!"

To me our guys did not seem afraid. They were ready to rock and roll wherever, whoever we played. I had heard the rumors about the Bulldogs making plans to knock my head around. I even received a few phone calls at night. But I felt sorry for my former teammates regardless of whether anyone hated me or not. They did not deserve that kind of treatment, going through so much.

One night a strange voice on the phone said, "Hey, mister concussion traitor, we gonna put you back in the hospital." I laughed it off and kept to my schedule. Coincidentally, The 'House had benefitted from the transfer of Billy Vassar, a Peabody student who had shifted to Westinghouse at the same time as my opposite transfer. Billy was an intimidating competitor who loved to call people out for a fight. He was also a great all- around ball player, who played all sports with great intensity. Maybe he should have been a boxer because of his extra-large hands and big head. I remembered him from last year as the Highlanders' defensive corner. His tackles were hard, clean and well done. We would have to play hard ourselves and as one unit to overcome Billy and the Bulldogs.

It was a crazy week. Two days before the big game, the hype spilled over into East Liberty and nearby neighborhoods, like Garfield and the Peabody end of Larimer Avenue. During practice our stands were filled with all kinds of people, including many adults. A few looked somewhat shady, jumping in and out of a long black Cadillac. Folks were placing bets on the game. People cheered as we made our way on and off the practice field.

Some of our players were beginning to get nervous about our Friday afternoon battle. Johnny Yandell and Dave Gerasole first recognized the shaky ones. A short, well-built Italian kid, Dave was the Highlanders' captain and starting guard. Davey kept the Italians, Jews and Slavic kids from acting up. Johnny, who played both offense and defense and never hesitated to point out our shortcomings, kept the brothers in check by joking away any racial tension before it started. Jim Levey, our quarterback, made direct appeals to the Jewish kids to join in the unity of our team. Together the threesome ironed out problems before each game.

Pres Robinson and his buddy James Boyd were our cheerleader players. They started a tradition of singing the "Limbo Rock" by Chubby Checker every day at the top of their voices. In the shower after practice they'd start and everyone joined in. Louder and louder we sang until our ears almost exploded. The "Limbo Rock" was our unity theme, our invitation for blacks, whites, Jews, Italians, Greeks, Irish, and others to become one, naked in the shower, singing one song and standing with each other as a team.

On Wednesday after practice our spirits needed a lift. Dave Gerasole walked into the middle of our locker room. He scanned the room, intense, prepared to tell us something. We all fell silent.

"Two days from now we are going to play The 'House. They want our butts pretty bad, I hear. I don't care if you're white or black, Jewish or Italian, we have not come this far together to lay down for eleven kids who put their pants on same way we do. I'll be damned if I chicken out. We can beat these guys if we stay together." He got louder: "Yandell, get the brothers together. Jim Levey, get the Jews together. John Leone, have a meeting with all the dagos." By now he was demanding: "Tomorrow, last practice, I don't want to see nobody walking with their heads down afraid."

We all clapped and cheered Dave's speech. Everyone was pumped. I looked over at Johnny Yandell, who winked his left eye. He was up to something.

"What was that wink about, man?" I asked him later as we started walking home down Highland.

"Some of them chucks are still scared, man," he said with a devilish look. "We got to get our key players even madder by Friday. I think Jim Gentile is our man. He faces big House Hardy on the line. Man, House is so big and so mean, he could destroy our entire offense."

"How do you plan to stop him?"

"Simple, with Gentile."

Gentile was only five-foot-six, but he weighed over 240. His neck was 22 inches around. Johnny thought that all we had to do was get Gentile pissed off at big House.

"And how do we do that?" I asked the twinkle in Johnny's eyes.

"Call him up tonight, tell him you're House, and say if Jimmy shows up for the game you're gonna beat his mama up. Italians love their mamas. He will go crazy on House. I already told him House has a bad knee."

"Man, I don't sound like House," I said.

"Don't worry, it will be taken care of, man." John concluded his plan with his loud, signature shot of a laugh.

Thursday after practice Jimmy Gentile was banging his head on the metal lockers: ready to play.

That Friday, mid-afternoon was sunny and bright as our bus passed under the tunnel down to the Westinghouse field. Everyone was excited. Small groups of Bulldog and Highlander cheerleaders jumped up and down as we parked. I could see a few of my former classmates laughing and pointing our way. Already suited up, we left the bus and assembled overlooking their field. I quickly suppressed my memories of many hard runs up and down the long embankment at my feet. I watched my teammates looking down on that sad, substandard field, where the off-season pitcher's mound raised a hump on its south side. Not even a water fountain, like the one at one end of the Peabody field. A ragged shack and a couple of football sleds.

The bleachers were full of Bulldog fans. On a distant hill-side people were standing, sitting and running around tossing a miniature football. The Silver Lake Drive-In, from which you could look up and see the field, was packed with cars and fans wearing Peabody colors, maroon and gray. Other shouting, waving fans were perched on the Lincoln Avenue bridge and the railroad bridge, which also gave them a view of the game. It was an awesome sight. The air was electric. The fans went mad as both teams assembled on the field.

Somewhere in the madness of that moment before kick-off, my mind slipped into a zone. I could not see, hear, or taste anything but those hundred brown gridiron yards.

The game began. Our cleats dug in, helmets clashed and pads shuddered with every hit. The sheer force of our defense gained respect even from the Bulldog fans. Gentile kept banging big House Hardy's knees so bad he hobbled off the Bulldogs' defense.

For both sides there was no tomorrow. Billy Vassar smashed Mike Telakis in the backfield several times on Mike's fullback runs. My old track buddy Orin Richburg was extremely fast but very light in the hips, and several times I tossed him into the stands.

Both teams scored. We also both missed the extra point. By the fourth quarter they had taken a 12-6 lead. After that, our defense held them off and caused them to fumble near our own goal line. We recovered, but then they stopped us on their thirty-two.

Time was running out. Twice they tried to run up the middle. Then they decided to do what few, if any, 'House teams ever tried. Coach Meyers saw it coming, warning Johnny and me to watch for a pass. The ball was snapped to their fullback, Spider and, sure enough, he handed it off to their quarterback, Hindu, for the throw. Meanwhile, their right end, Bootsey Goodson, ran down and out to the sideline. Hindu threw for Bootsey and was intercepted by Yandell. My blocks on Hindu and Spider sprang big John loose to dance into their end zone. Our native-German kicker, Aldo Zortea, trotted on and kicked the extra point. Minutes later the final gun sounded. We had just defeated Coach Reno's mighty Westinghouse Bulldogs on their home turf.

All hell broke loose. The state of shock among the thousands of Bulldog fans quickly turned to rage. Hundreds were crying and embracing each other. Many of the Bulldogs' most loyal fans rolled on the ground to express their sorrow. One kid dressed in a Sunday suit rolled madly around in a patch of oil beside the field.

Before long, fights broke out on the field, the nearby hillside and even the grounds of the Silver Lake Drive-In. Hundreds of kids were kicked and stomped on. The stadium had gone totally mad. And there we were, smack in the middle. Rocks and bottles were flew everywhere. Coach Meyers told us to put our helmets back on and run for the bus, and somehow all our players made it.

"Get away from those windows!" he yelled.

Someone shouted, "Lay on the floor and cover your face!"

The rioters gathered around our bus, rocking it, blocking its path, shouting, screaming our names. Inside, two guys were cut by flying glass as every window was broken. I could see who these mad people were. Some of them had been my friends from as far back as grade school. I was shocked to see the hatred on their swollen faces. It was like they'd never known me at all. Some evil had transformed these good and reasonable people into raving fools. The loss had unleashed demons I had never seen. In that moment I wondered whether they'd ever been true friends at all. I guessed they'd valued our friendship only because I'd played for The 'House.

Sirens blared. Police cars came from everywhere. A squad of policemen pushed the rioters away from our bus. We began to move toward home. As we rolled away down Frankstown, large crowds of fans kept rioting. They beat up pedestrians, stoned parked cars and broke the windows of many businesses.

Finally we arrived back at Peabody. Everyone started to celebrate by singing our "Limbo Rock." Thousands of Highlander fans were waving maroon-and-gray banners, cheering and jumping with joy as the team piled off the bus.

Mr. Paul Williams, the only black teacher I recall being at Peabody then, pulled Johnny Yandell and me to the side.

"Hey guys, great game. I loved it," he said. "But we have received threats on your lives, and I know you live in Homewood. Right now it isn't safe for either of you to walk those streets, so we're getting the police to escort you home."

Johnny and I looked at each other and laughed. Johnny said, "Oh, ah, Vera Wells lives in Homewood, also." Vera was a cheerleader.

Mr. Williams nodded. "Then the police will take her home, too. Exactly where do you all live?"

A short while later, after we managed to shower and change, he jumped in the front of a waiting police car. Vera hopped in the back seat with Johnny and me. She was very pretty, always wearing her long black hair in a single, thick braid down the back. She was light-coffee brown with large shining eyes that complemented her pleasant smile. We headed back toward Homewood. Half way home, she yelled and leaned forward clutching her knee.

Mr. Williams turned around. "What's wrong, Vera? Are you hurt?"

"I'm sorry, I got some kind of cramp in my leg." She was trying to hold back the tears.

"I'll fix that," said Johnny and started to massage her thighs.

Mr. Williams faked a cough. "Vera, we are almost on Mt. Vernon," he reassured her. "Try to hold on."

"Thanks, Mr. Williams," she said faintly.

Johnny and I smiled. Her cramp did take our minds off all the activity we passed on the way home. After we dropped off Vera, we all laughed loudly over Johnny's willingness to stroke her thighs. A short while later, he and I were dropped in front of our homes.

I still could not believe all my friends had turned on me. I waited for the police car to leave and headed toward Mary Lou's on Bennett. I arrived and was greeted by her mother, who had been laughing and teasing her daughter, who was crying in the kitchen.

"I'm glad you all beat them Bulldogs, John." Mrs. Brown gave me a pat on the back.

Her husband just sat in the corner of their small living room jamming snuff in his mouth. He rocked back and forth in his chair until the large wad disappeared behind his lips. He winked at me and continued to rock.

Suddenly, Mary Lou ran out of the kitchen with a butcher knife, screaming, "I hate you! I hate you!"

At first I thought she was joking so I played along like I was afraid. Before I knew it, her wild swings had me out the front door and onto the porch.

"Be cool, girl!" I said, but she kept on coming. I'd always known what a huge fan Mary Lou was of the Bulldogs, but I hadn't known she loved them more than anything, including me.

Behind me, other girls were screaming, "Get him, get him, girl! He's a traitor!" I turned and saw five angry girls in blue and gold. As kids on Baxter playground I had known them all. I couldn't win. I turned and dashed up the street toward home, which had to be the only place in Homewood that still welcomed my face.

Mom and Dad stood in our living room grinning broadly. My brothers were excited as well. Somehow these smiling faces made the pain and shocks of the day disappear.

Dad knew about the special police escort. He'd probably made the arrangements himself. I was invited into our dining room and treated to my favorite dinner. This was a special occasion. I could smell the almost heavenly aroma of steak, mashed potatoes and greens with relish on the side. Mom had even baked an apple pie that Dad was ready to top from a large bowl of our favorite, vanilla ice cream.

"Great game, boy," he said.

"Thanks, Dad." I felt like a king. "This is one day I'll never forget."

"Well, you achieved your goal to beat Cesare at his own game," he said. "How do you feel about that?"

"Great feeling, Dad, to bring him down." I paused. "But I saw some things today that really confused me, like all the kids I thought were my friends, all turning on me like dogs."

I almost sobbed.

"Don't worry son," he said. "If someone is a true friend, they won't let one football game come between you."

It took me a while to respond. "I guess you're right," I said at last, and went on to devour Mom's great dinner.

"So, today you have learned a valuable lesson about life, haven't you?" he said as he passed me the pie à la mode.

I nodded and smiled, enjoying the rest of that family evening.

The Final Challenge

One week later we played South Hills High. At last Coach Meyers put me in as starting fullback. But we played a miserable game and lost because we had still been celebrating our victory over The 'House. That loss to South Hills dumped us back in a three-way tie for first place in our division with Westinghouse and South Hills.

As the final gun sounded, Pres Robinson threw his helmet to the ground and said, "Damn!"

We dropped our heads. No "Limbo Rock" in the shower tonight.

"Where did we go wrong?" asked Vernon.

"Probably too much party time with the white girls last week," James said with a smile.

"Yeah, that was some kind of reception we got last Saturday," Pres agreed.

Our entire team had received open invitations to eat whatever we wanted at several East Liberty establishments. We ate free pizza. Some of the guys went to Broudy's and pigged out on Reuben sandwiches and pop. The parties were wild up in Stanton Heights, the heavily Jewish neighborhood, at some girl's house—a beer blast with plenty of girls running around to half-past-one in the morning.

Then all week we had dragged through practice thinking South Hills was in the bag. Wrong. But despite the loss our fans were still there to support us. Peabody's sports fans were mostly parents from the Parent Teacher Student Association. They were a strong, organized group who were fully involved in the school, and many of their kids had gone out for a team. There were business men, shop merchants, lawyers, and even big-time gangsters doing whatever they could to support us. They were different from the fans I had known, were with us whether we won or lost. We all appreciated that.

"You're still in first place, guys. Don't look so down," My buddy Steve said from the crowd.

Back at school the evening after South Hills, we walked into the locker room and sat for a while to reflect. The place was silent as a tomb.

Then John Leone shouted, "It ain't over until it's over!" He screamed it again and again and started shoving us around. John's tears rolling off his red face, his determination, touched us all.

Everyone stood up and repeated, "Ain't over until it's over!" James struck up our theme song as we stripped and gathered in the shower. We had lost a game but not the season.

Four days later, Tuesday afternoon, we learned that South Hills would be our opponent again in the first stage of play-offs. Pittsburgh's school board had announced that the games would be played at South Stadium as a way of preventing or controlling any rioting like what had happened after our game at The 'House. We had heard reports about hundreds of kids being injured after the game. Westinghouse area business owners also were filing suits to recover damages caused by the riot.

Coach Meyers never beat us up about winning or losing, but he made it a point to talk to us about the value of good sportsmanship. He was a humble man, truly dedicated to our personal development, not to his own winning record—confident in us but never bragging. We respected him and all knew what we had to do to honor him.

"Just do your best," he said to us now as he always did.

In the playoff we crushed South Hills. On one play, for example, Johnny Leone simply wiped out the middle of their defensive line. Icould have driven my dad's station wagon through the hole he had opened. Instead, I bolted through on a 66-yard, six-point dash. Moments later I intercepted a pass over a South Hills end and ran 33 yards for another easy score. We beat them just like they had beat us the week before.

But now it was time for Westinghouse vs. Peabody, final round. As the whole city knew, this was the Bulldogs' ticket to avenge a painful loss. During the week that preceded that second game, I bumped into two of my old teammates when Kendow and Little Mac popped their heads out of the Five & Ten on Homewood Avenue.

"Hey Bronco, you ready for the big game?" Little Mac asked.

"Yeah, I'm ready, man," I replied as confidently as I could.

Kendow looked back over his shoulder, then shook my hand. We walked down Homewood toward the park. He pulled a bottle of King Soloman out of his jacket.

"Want a hit, Bronco?"

I remembered our drinking days.

"Naw, man."

"Kendow, be cool," said Mac. "Stay off that stuff."

"So what's happening in The Room?" I asked.

Kendow lowered the bottle and said, "Reno went mad, man, after the loss. He acted like some fool. He cussed and blamed you and Johnny Yandell for leaving the community. He blamed Clyde Hefflin. He blamed Hindu most of all for throwing that interception. He was slobbering and spitting all over us. "

Kendow could do funny imitations. His Reno Cesare impersonation made Little Mac and me laugh until our sides began to hurt. Then Mac's look turned into one of concern.

"Hey, Bronco, better watch out. He wants you hurt, man. They were talking about hitting you in the head and bringing those concussions."

"I'm not worried about that," I lied and changed the subject to the wild scenes after the last game between us.

Kendow laughed. "Did you see Joey Avent roll on the ground in his new gray suit?"

"Yeah," said Mac, "and we heard about your girl trying to knife you in the back. Is that girl crazy or what?"

I said, "Everyone was crazy that day."

"Well," said Kendow, "we better split up before some big mouth sees us together. Reno don't want us to even speak to anybody but Bulldogs. Everything's changed now, man. Guys see him for what he really is. Reno don't give a shit about us, man. The janitor showed me a letter from a college out west that wanted to see some films of my games. Reno tossed the letter in the trash. I wonder, how many other letters like that one has he canned over the years?"

He heaved the wine bottle into the bushes.

I commiserated as well as I could, telling him how I had already received ten letters from schools mailed directly to Peabody.

"Every week Mr. Z hands me a letter from some big school," I said. "At this rate I'll have twenty offers this year. I never got one at Westinghouse last year after making all-city and MVP. I know Cesare tossed out letters meant for me."

We shook hands and parted, me feeling good all over that my two oldest buddies and I were still solid. I really appreciated our long and honest talk and thought about how our next meeting would be as fierce opponents on the field.

Two days before the big game, Coach Meyers instructed the trainer to place more padding inside my specially designed helmet. Now I could barely hear Jim Levey call out signals. The problem was that at middle linebacker and at fullback I had to be able to hear every sound, and I wanted to hear and see in advance whoever was aiming to take my head off. Secretly, I removed the padding.

Finally our big day arrived and the Highlanders met The 'House again, this time on neutral ground at South. Play after play, I heard Bulldogs saying, "Hit him in the head!" But it really did not matter. We chewed up yardage and held theirs down and were rewarded with scoring first. Our kicker, Aldo, added the extra point. It was our only TD that day. The Bulldogs later scored on us, but we held them off from scoring more, just like they held off us. When the final quarter ended, we were tied at 7 to 7.

Both teams stood mid-field waiting for further instructions. The fans on both sides were also confused. The judges looked to a stadium tower.

Then a high-pitched P.A. system attempted to get our attention. The hidden speaker cleared his voice and announced, "Ladies and gentlemen, after reaching an end to regulation time, we have a 7 to 7 tie. There will be no overtime."

The stands cut him off with a chorus of boos.

"Instead, ...instead," he resumed as the boos let up, "we will come to a final decision by the penetration system. The judges will total up each team's number of first downs. The team with the most first downs is the winner."

The fans calmed down. We all stood waiting.

Then the voice came on again: "Westinghouse Bulldogs,... seven first downs."

The Bulldogs and fans jumped up and yelled.

"Peabody Highlanders... the Highlanders have.... nine first downs. The winner in this contest is Peabody High School."

The loudspeaker went dead. The Bulldogs stood there, silent, motionless as we ran off the field to celebrate. The police began to escort the fans out from the stands on either side.

Both teams had battled it out to the end, but we were the ones who'd made real history in Western Pennsylvania high school sports. Our last game that year, the city championship game against Langley, went our way like taking candy from a baby. The following Tuesday's *Pittsburgh Post-Gazette* ran our team photo under the caption, "Here's Peabody High's 1962 City League grid champs."

A little later that fall, Dad and I attended a Pitt vs. UCLA game at Pitt stadium. Dad was quick to point out that UCLA was probably the last college team in the country using a single-wing formation.

"And this will probably be the last year *anybody* uses it," he said as we watched the players line up. "Oh, ah, Butch I forgot to mention to you, it's definite now: this is the last year for students in the city not to have the option to attend whatever high school they want. I think this open enrollment will put old Reno pretty much out of business." He grinned and added, "Butch, there is always more than one way to skin a cat. Say, why don't you get us a couple of dogs and some pop."

He handed me a fresh five-dollar bill.

"Okay, Dad, be right back." I ran up the steps. "Four hot dogs and two pops, please," I asked the lady at the concession.

She filled my order. I turned to run back down to our seats and there behind me was Coach Reno Matthew Cesare, looking at me with eyes of hate. His teeth were grinding. He mumbled something I could not understand.

I smiled at him and said, "How's your Room now?"

In that moment, we both understood that one dirty gray door was soon to be shut forever. He melted into the crowd and we never crossed paths again.

Author's Note

The Room is a memoir of the betrayal of a group of young athletes in the past. I hope it will speak to young athletes and their coaches and mentors today in the face of similar problems.

The cover photo shows the Westinghouse Bulldogs fighting for yardage in 1958. The ball carrier on the back is Skippy Calloway. On the front, the nearest blocker is Bob Marshall. Behind him, blocking straight ahead, is Ralph Young.

Thanks to Arthur Davis, Rudy Dean and other former players who helped me verify the truth of my remembrances. In these pages I've changed a few names, but not those of my many past teammates and friends. I wish I could have mentioned them all individually.

Thanks to my folks for allowing me to travel my own path, especially to Dad for guiding me from a distance that always made me feel independent and strong. Thanks also to my Uncle James, Henry Yandell, Clyde Hefflin, and many others who freely gave me and my fellow players their own valuable hours, showing us the right way in sports.

I thank my good friend John Edgar Wideman for a great writer's insights about the book.

I thank Alan Venable, without whose passion for the story, encouragement, skillful editing, and publishing sweat, you would not be reading this account. Although this is not a work of fiction, I also thank novelist Margaret Murray for key storytelling suggestions and graphic designer Andrew Ogus for perceptive cover advice.

Last by not least, I thank my loving wife, Tina, who encouraged me to bring this story out again, first penned some thirty years ago, to share with our children Kristine and John, and you.

www.ingramcontent.com/pod-product-compliance
Lightning Source LLC
LaVergne TN
LVHW091004080826
845145LV00003B/1128

* 9 7 8 0 9 7 7 7 0 8 2 4 6 *